Zifflin's Coloring Book

Doodle Fusion

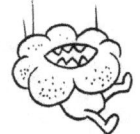

Hand Drawn Illustrations By Lei Melendres

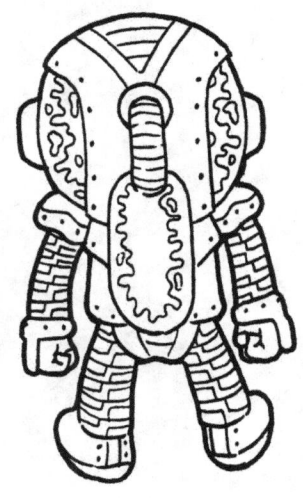

ISBN: 1517376912
ISBN-13: 978-1517376918

Zifflin's
Previous
Colorbook titles:

Doodle Invasion 2013
Doodle Realm 2014

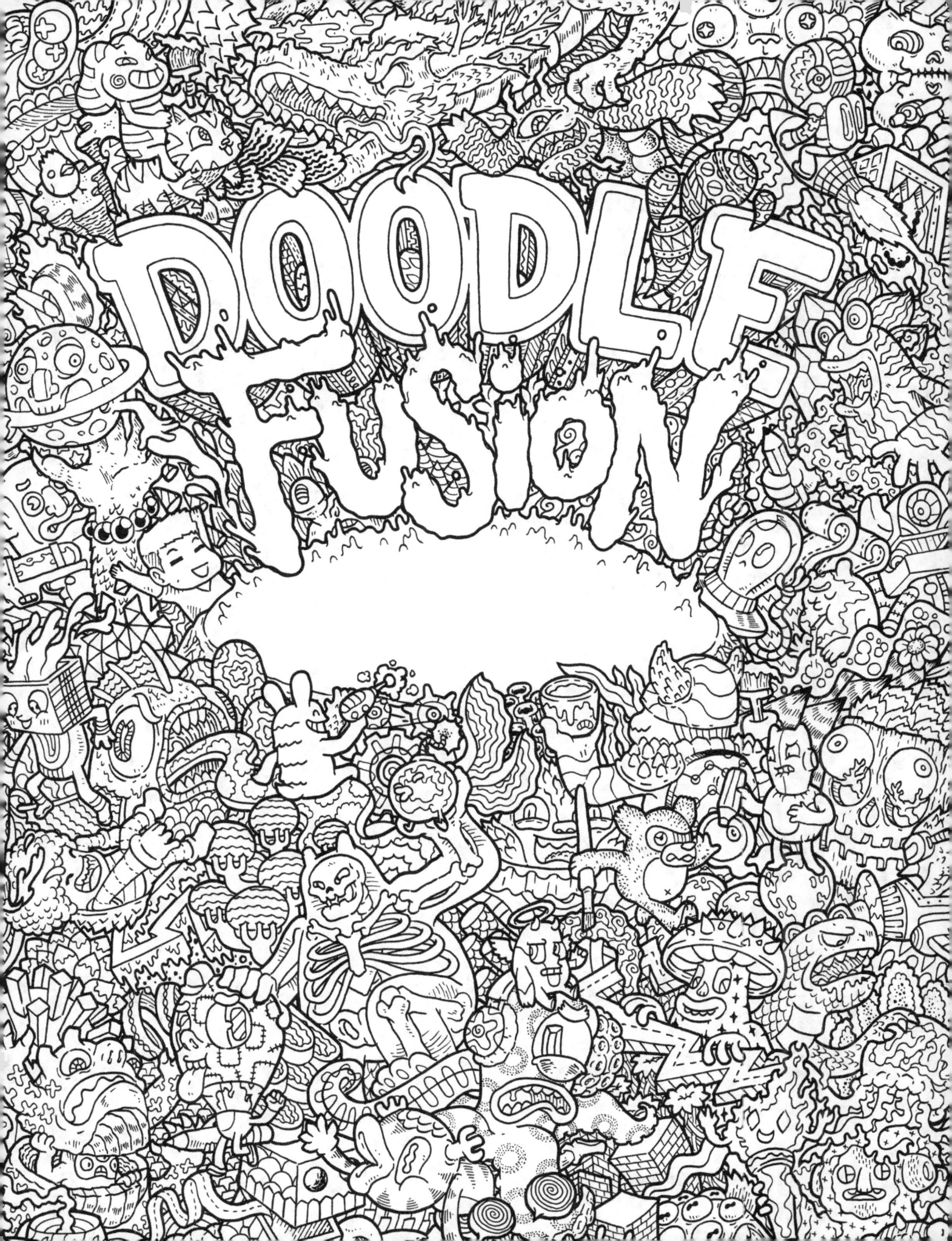

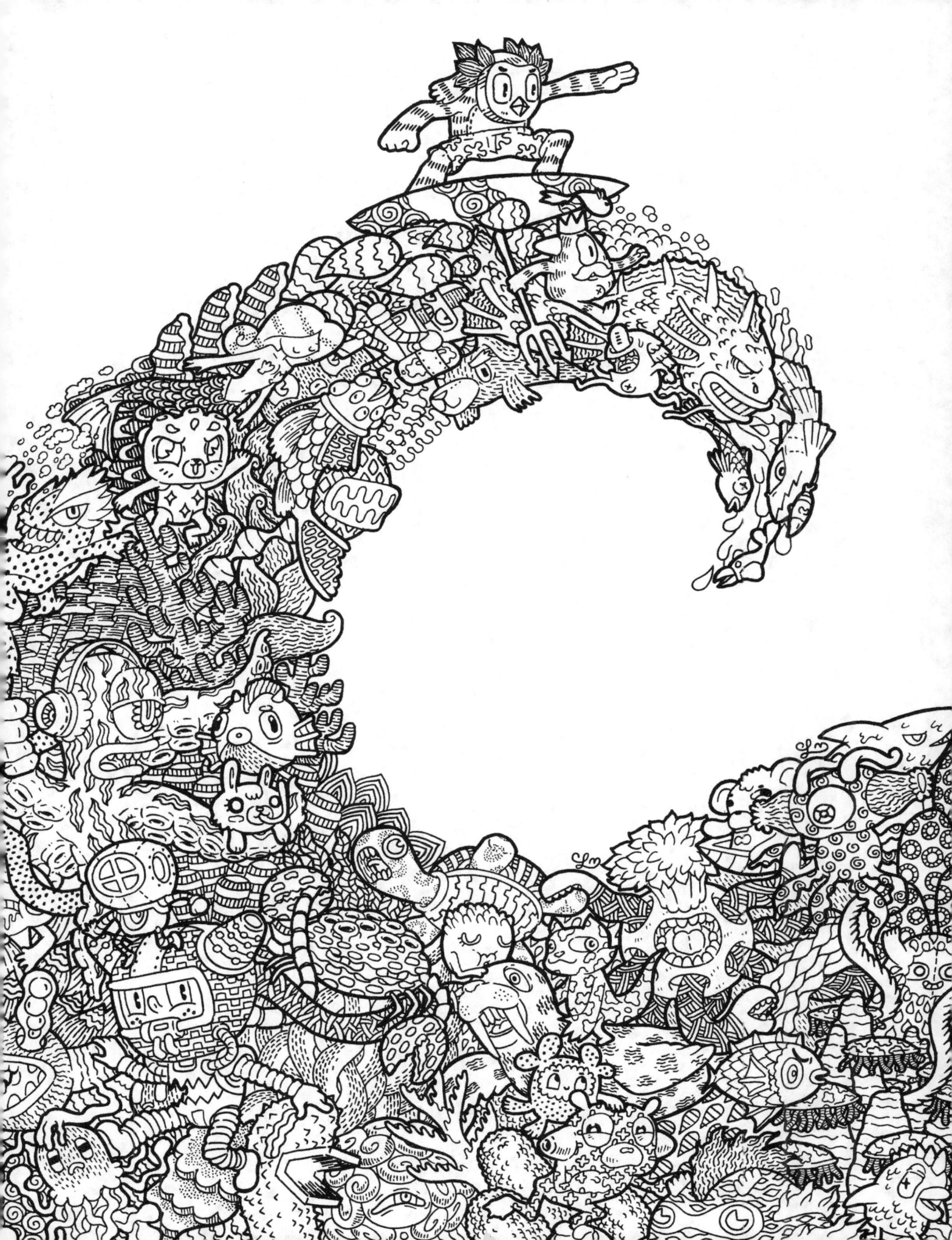

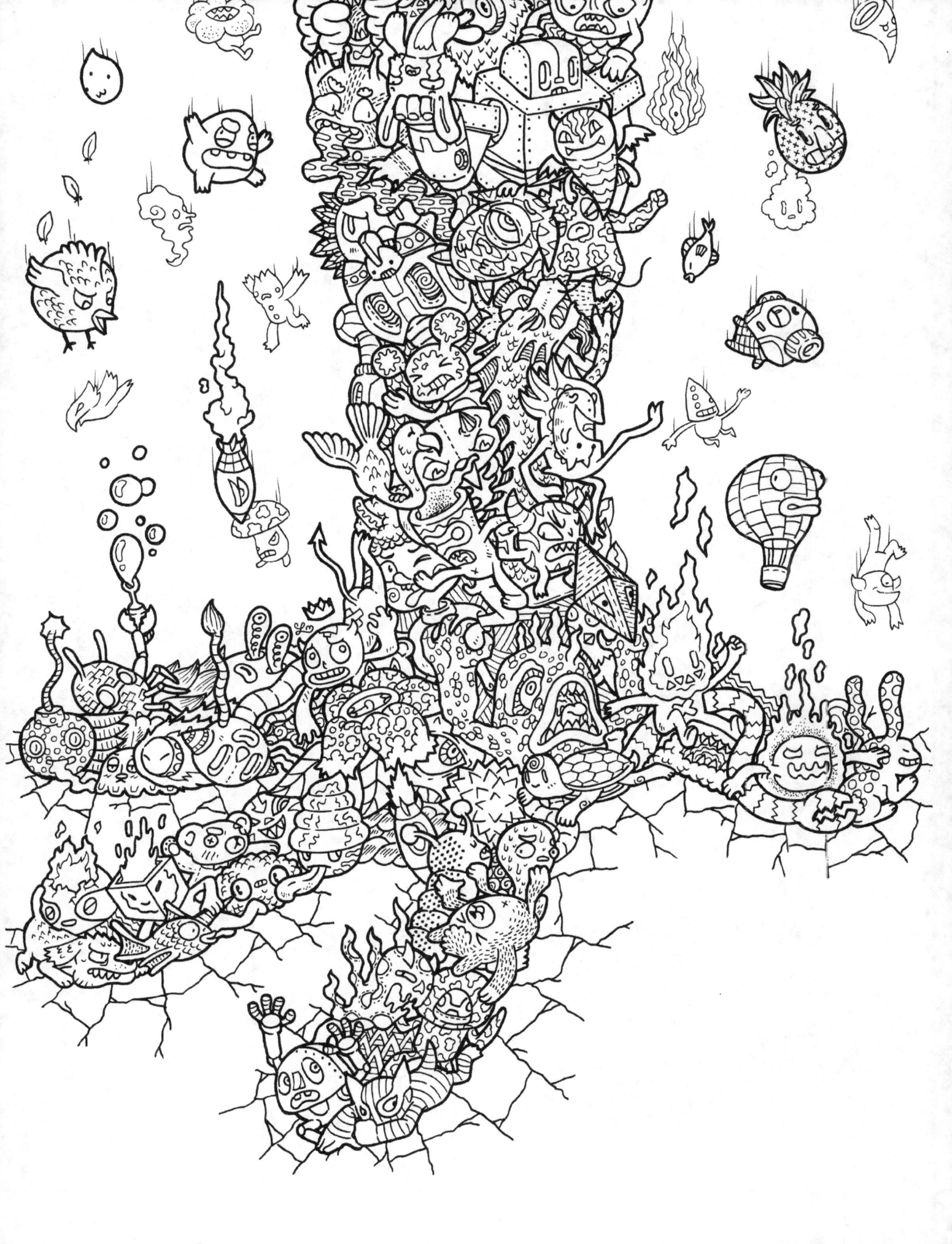

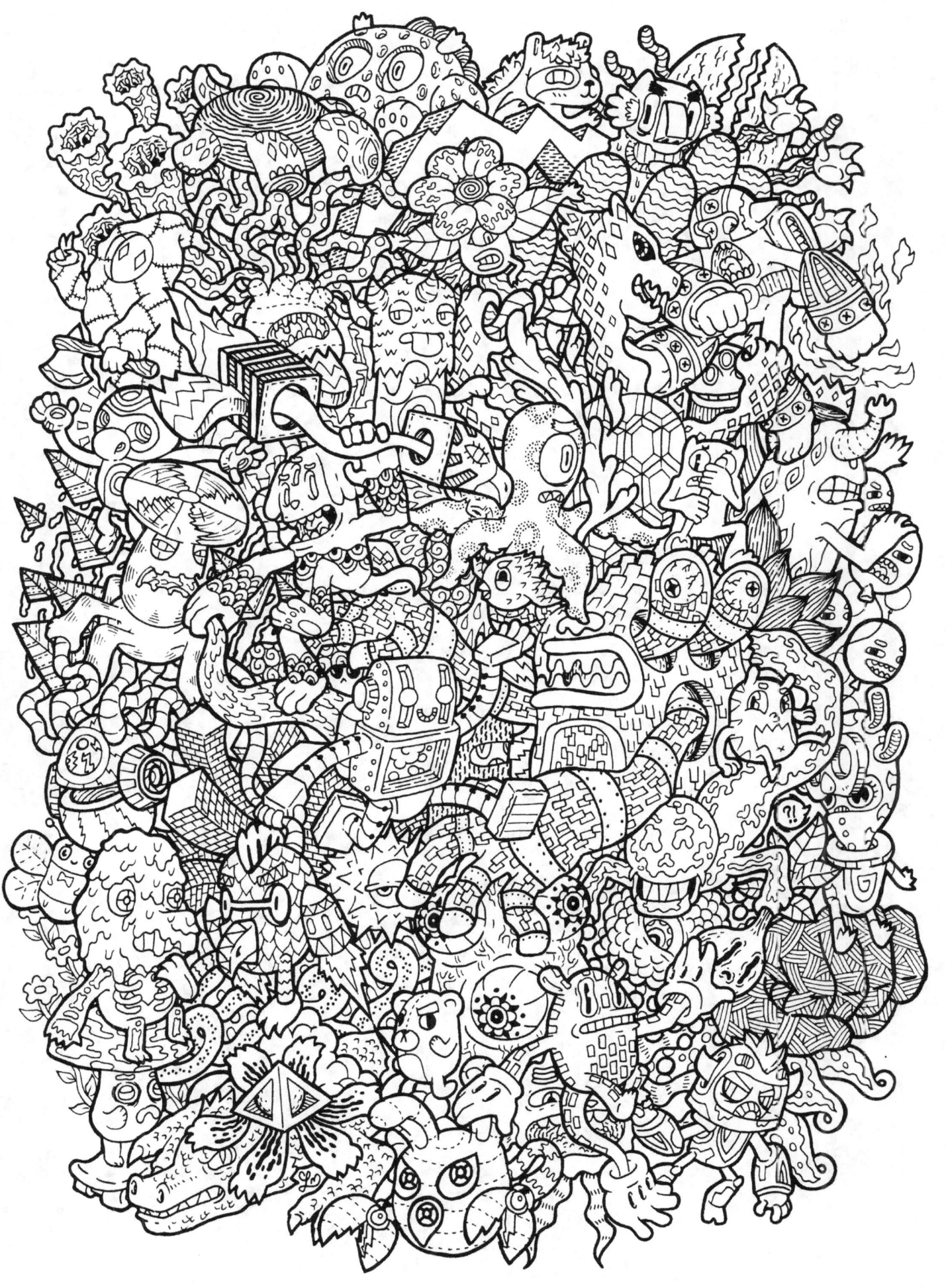

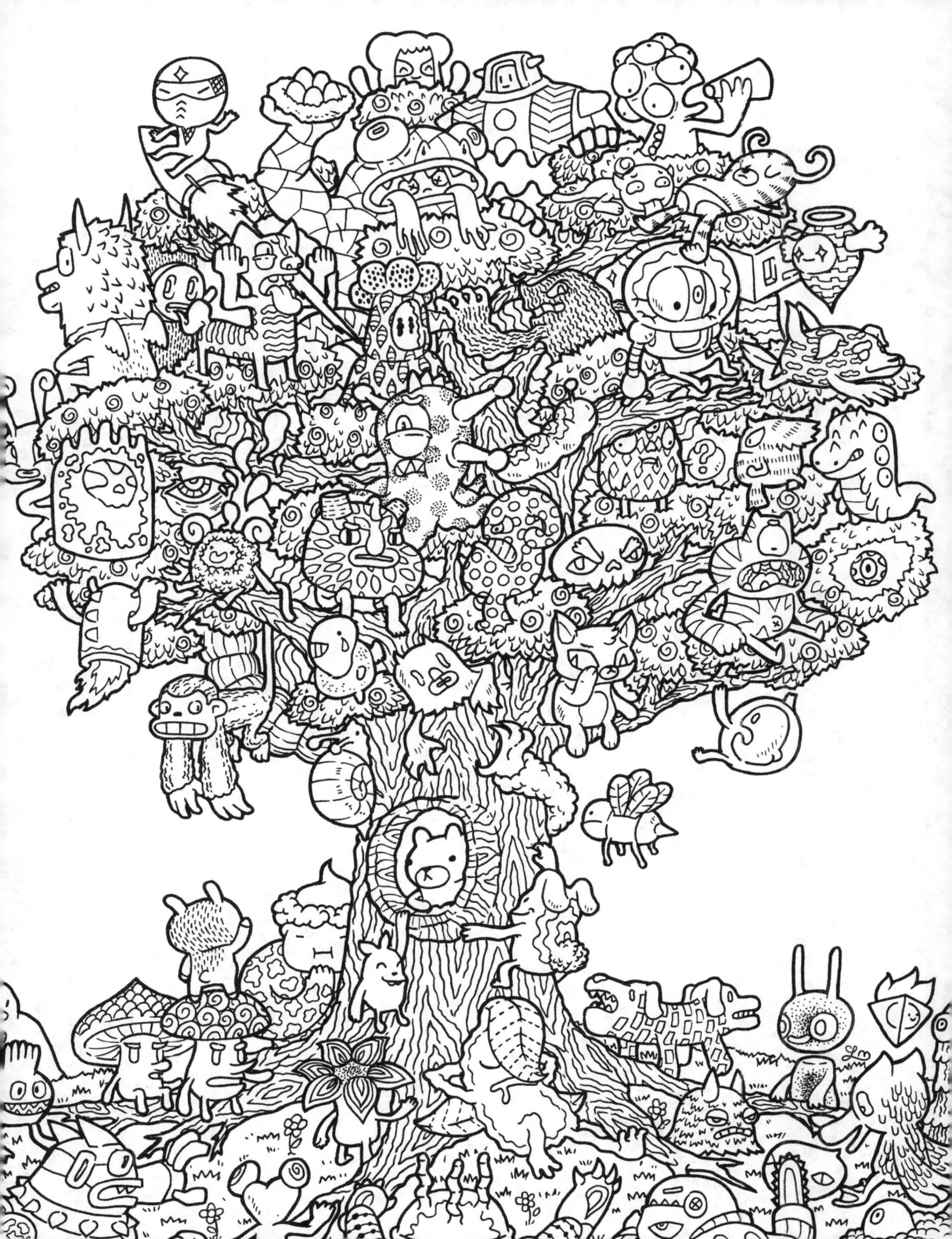

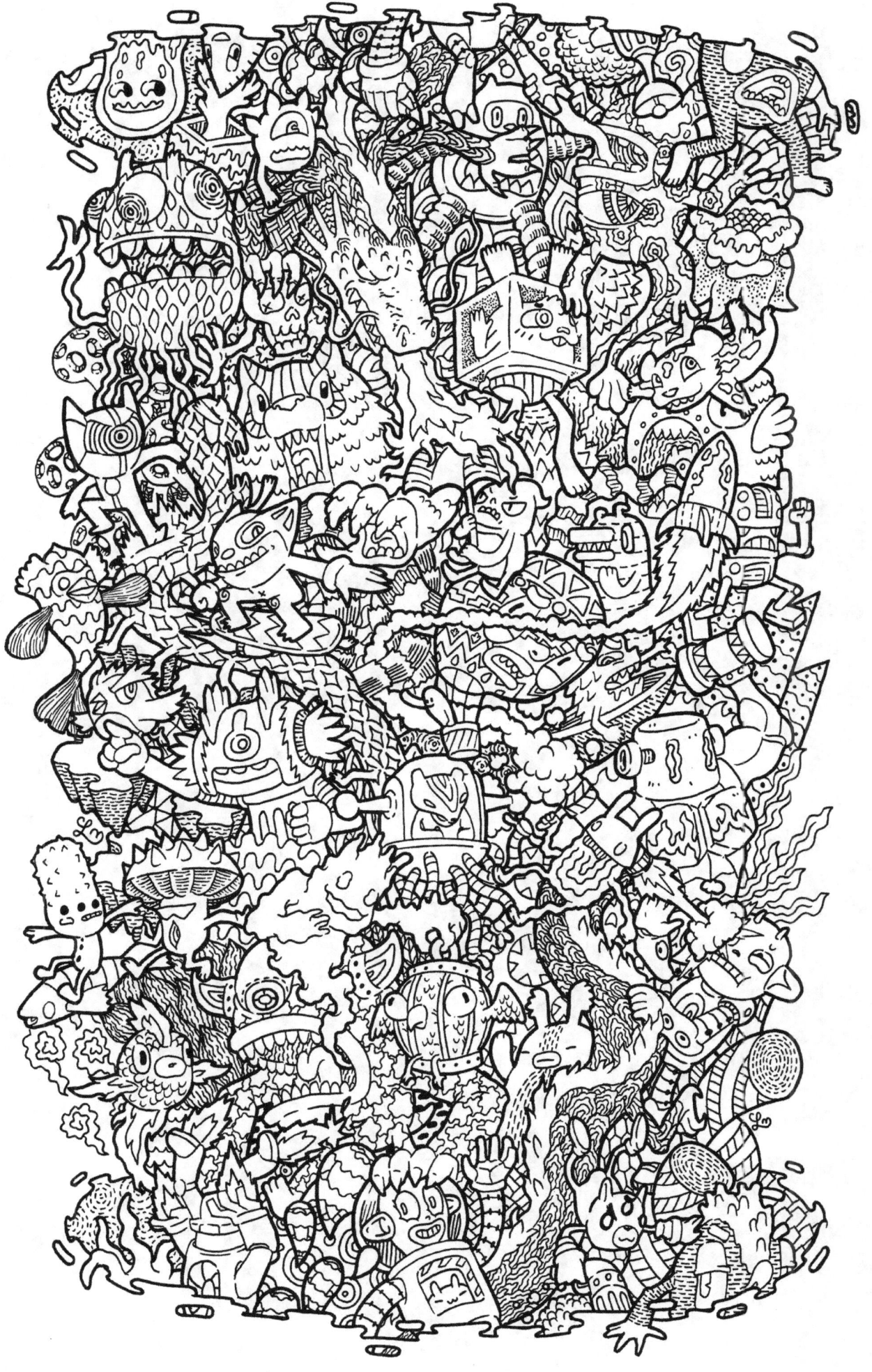

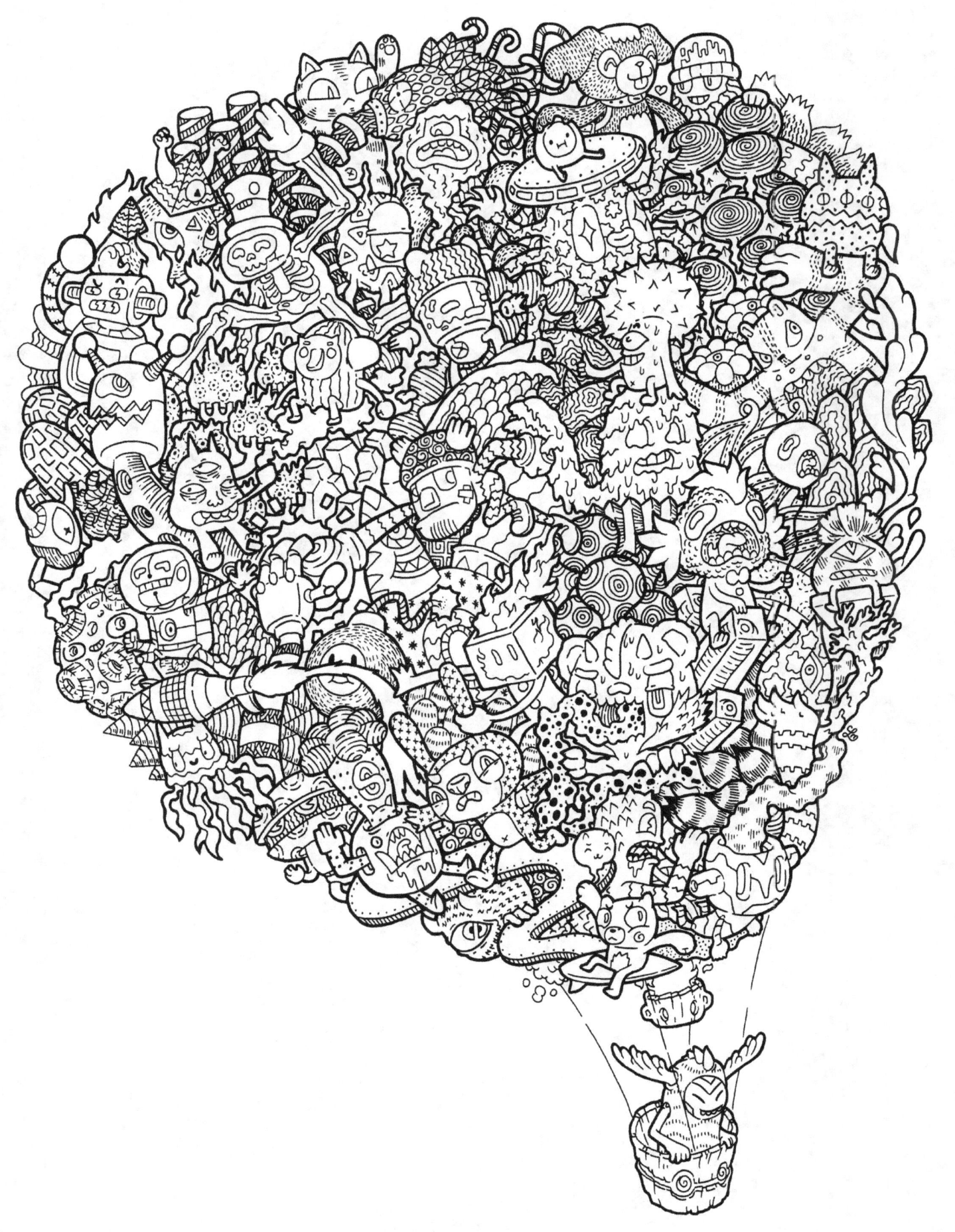

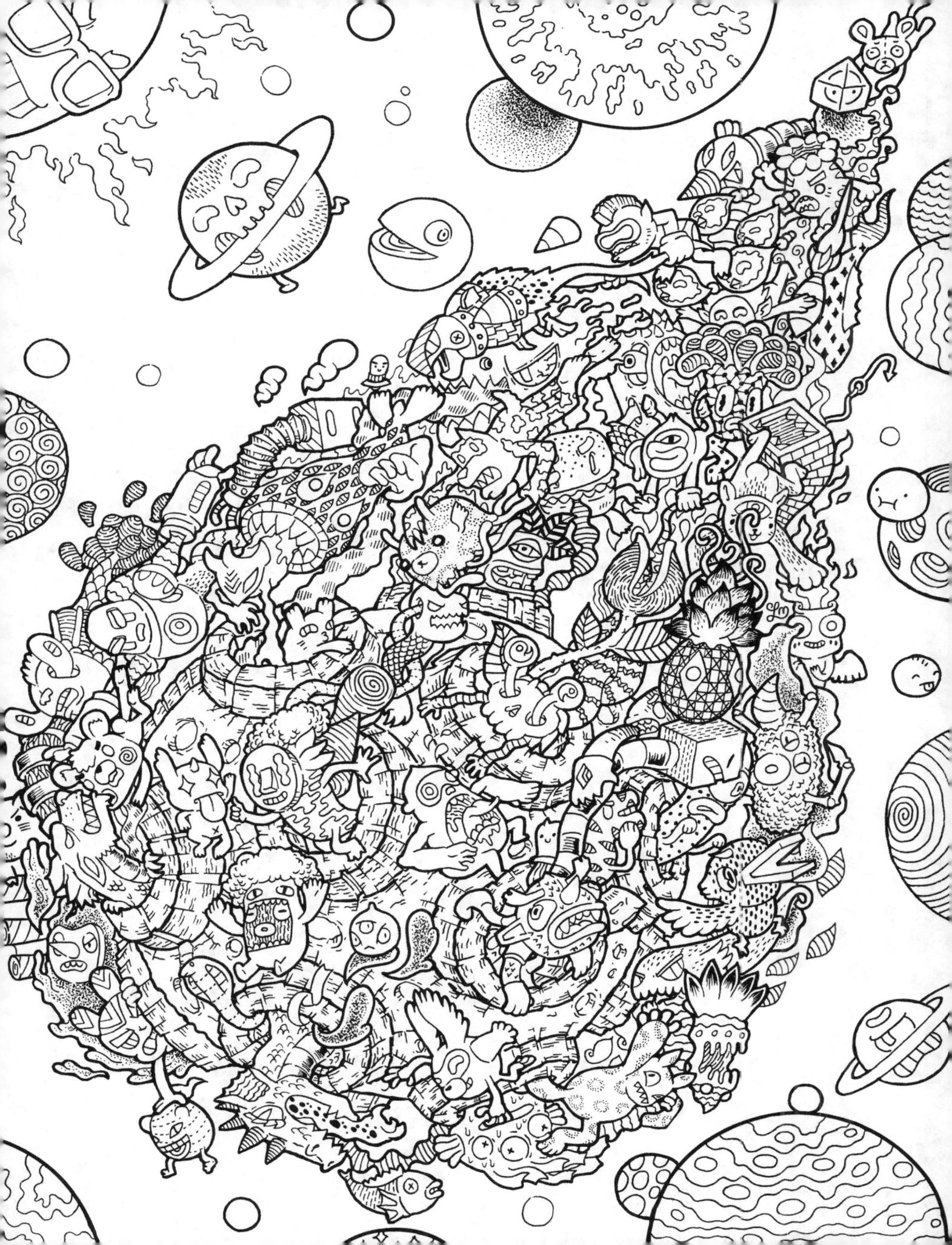

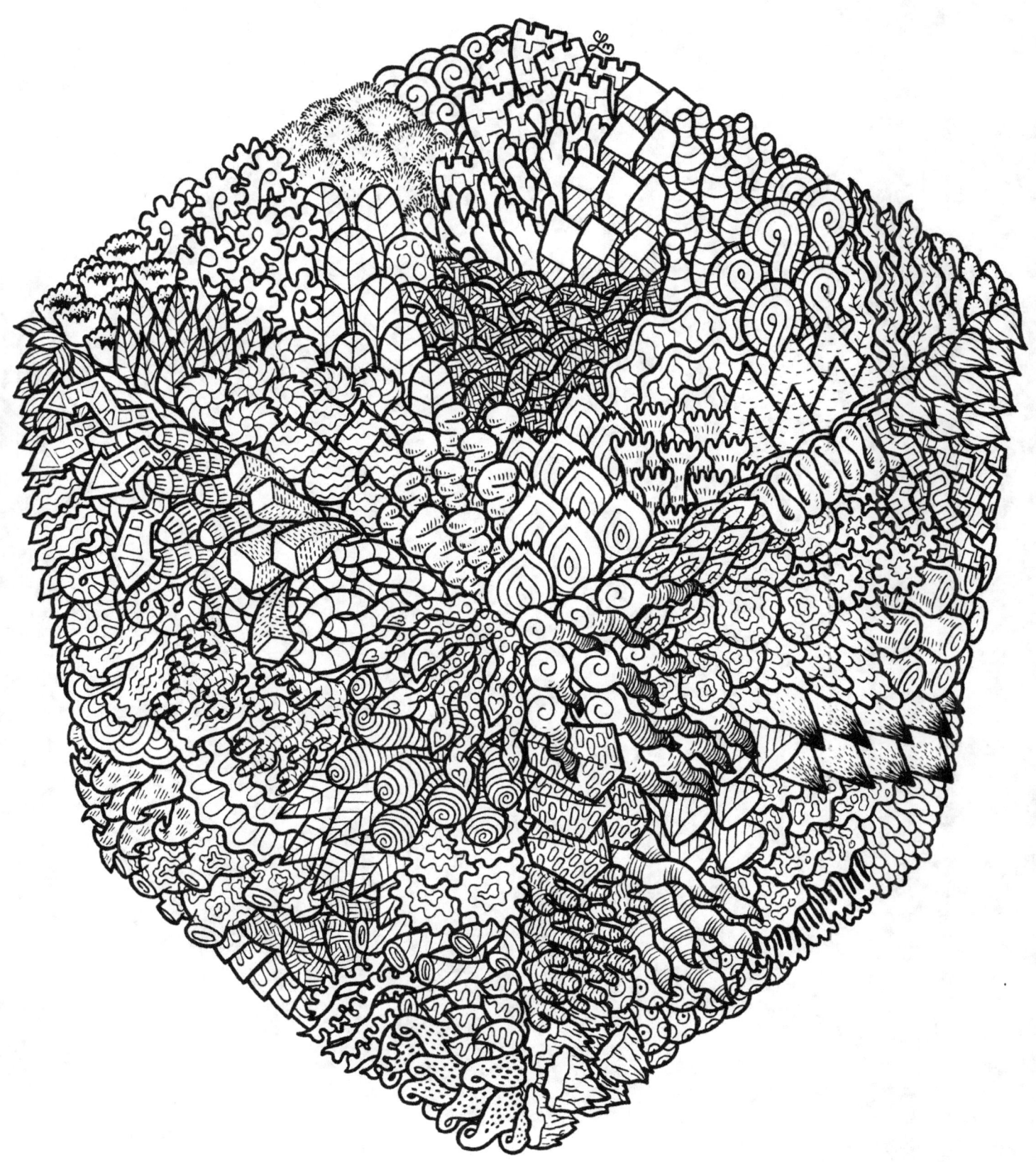

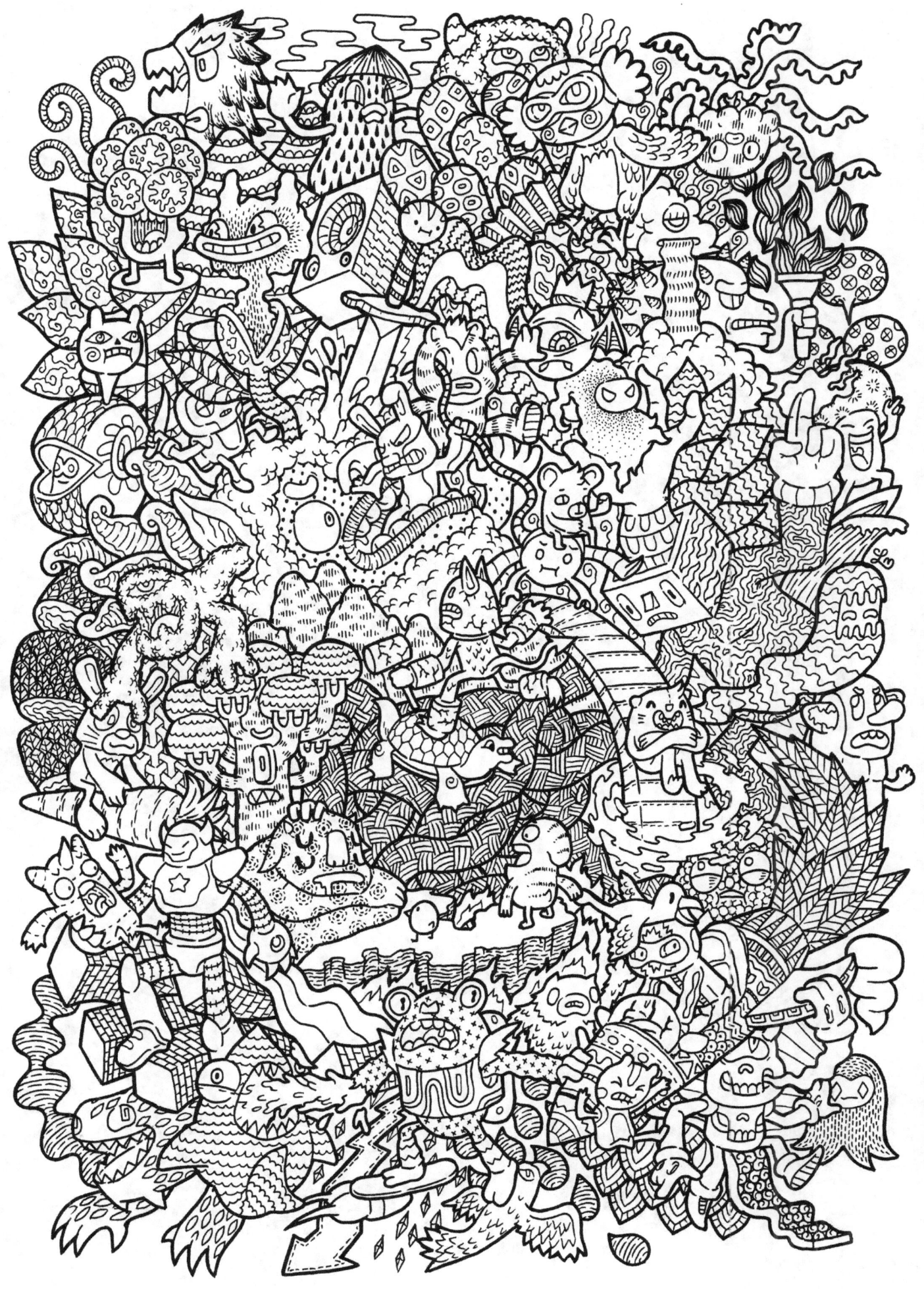

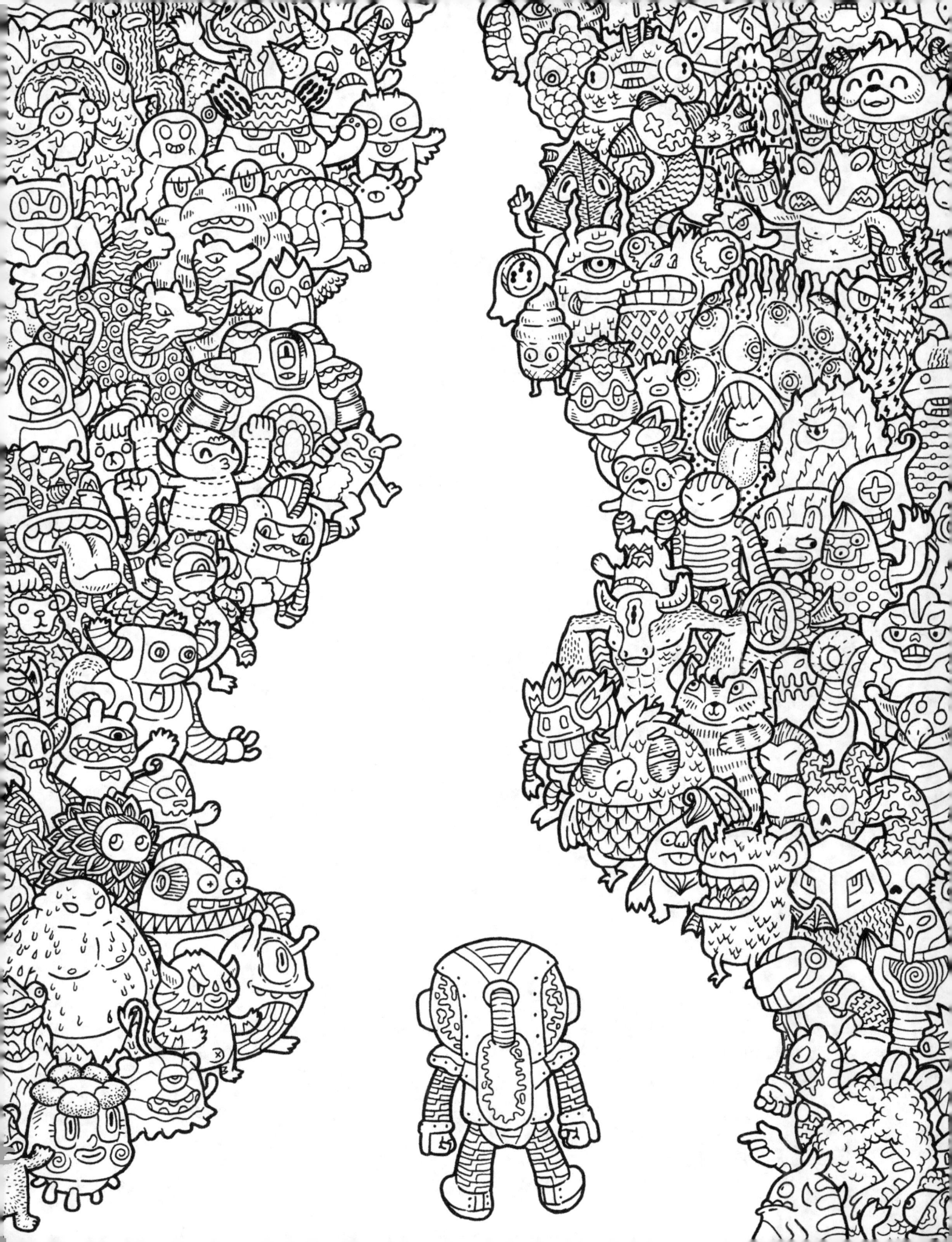

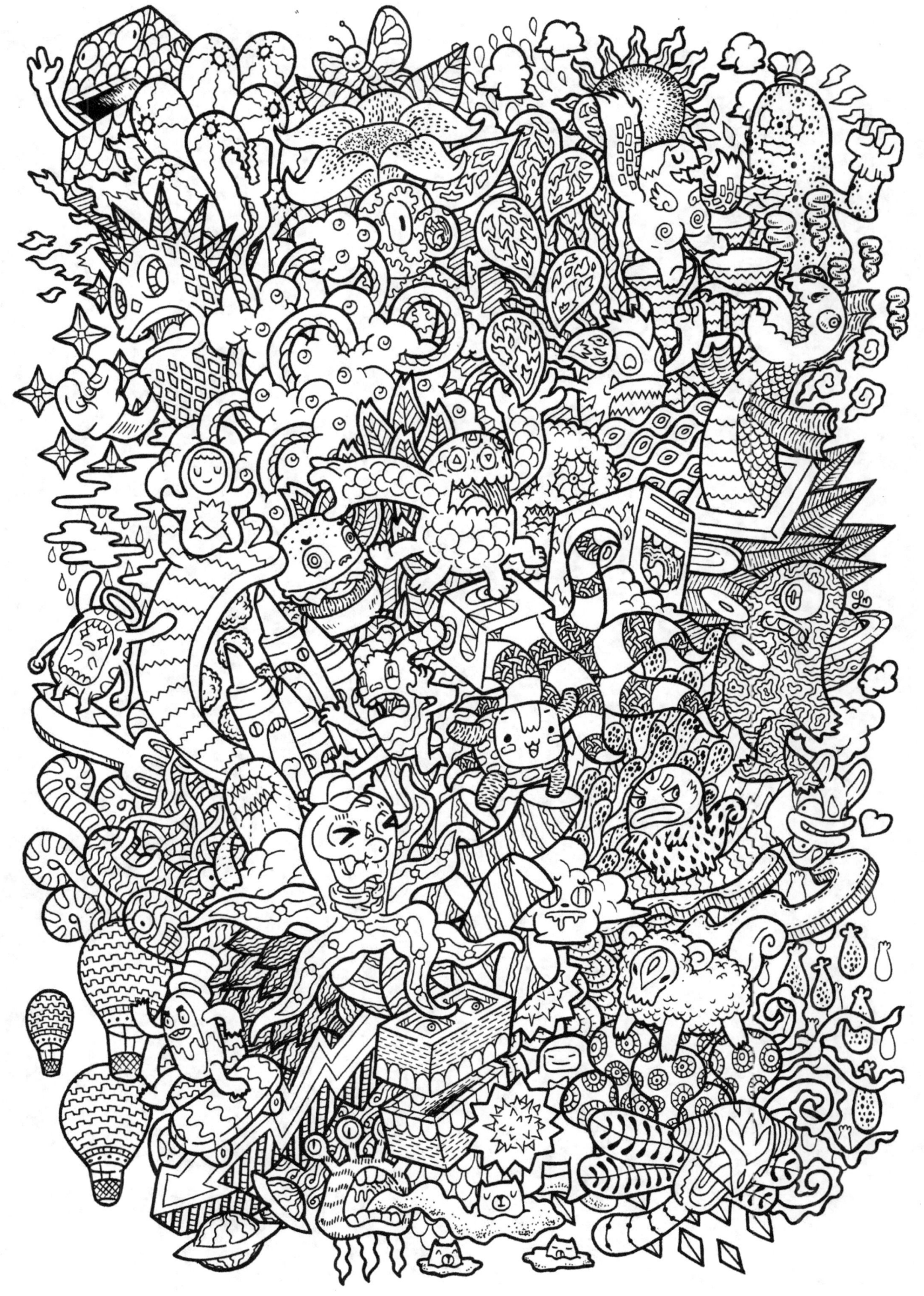

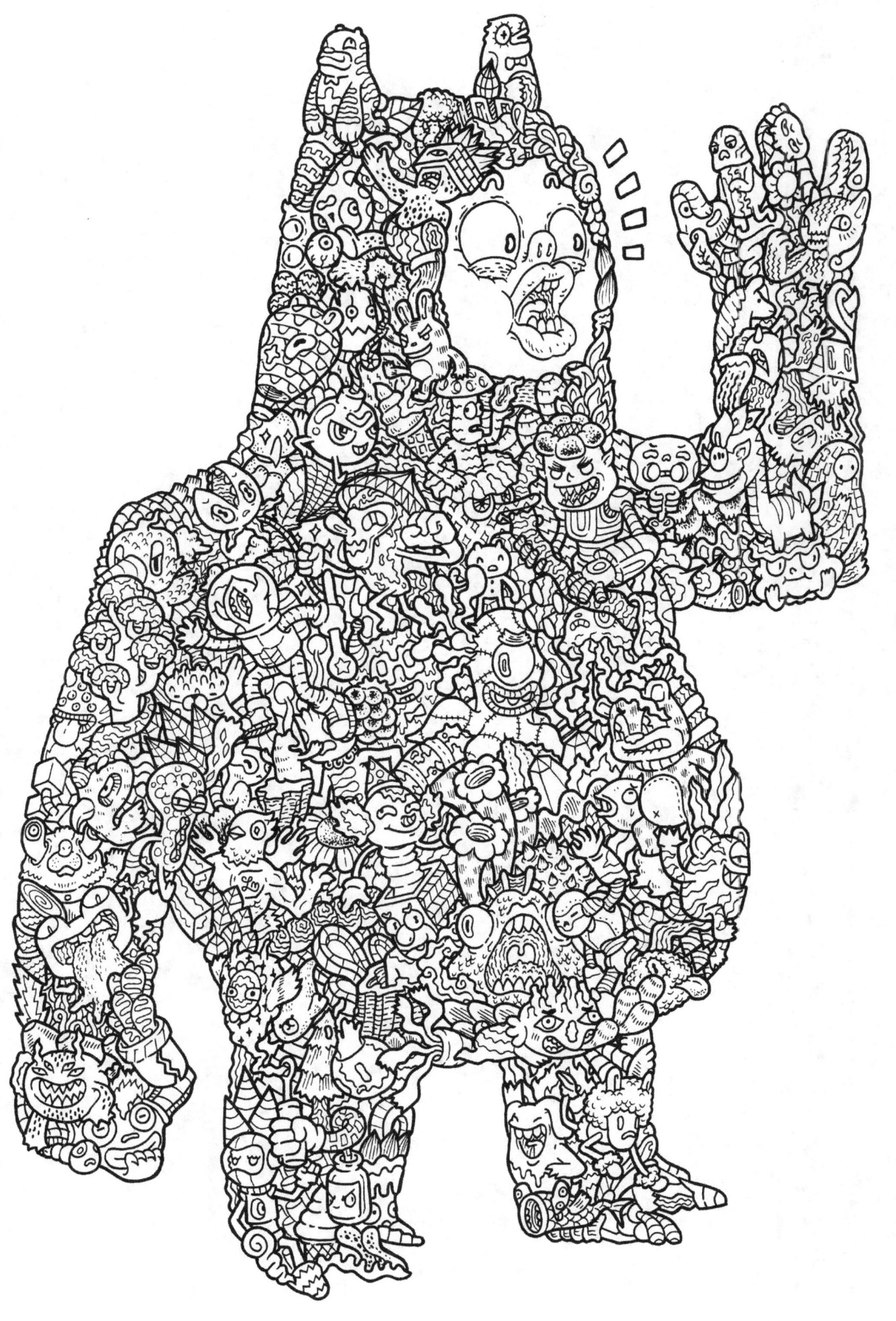

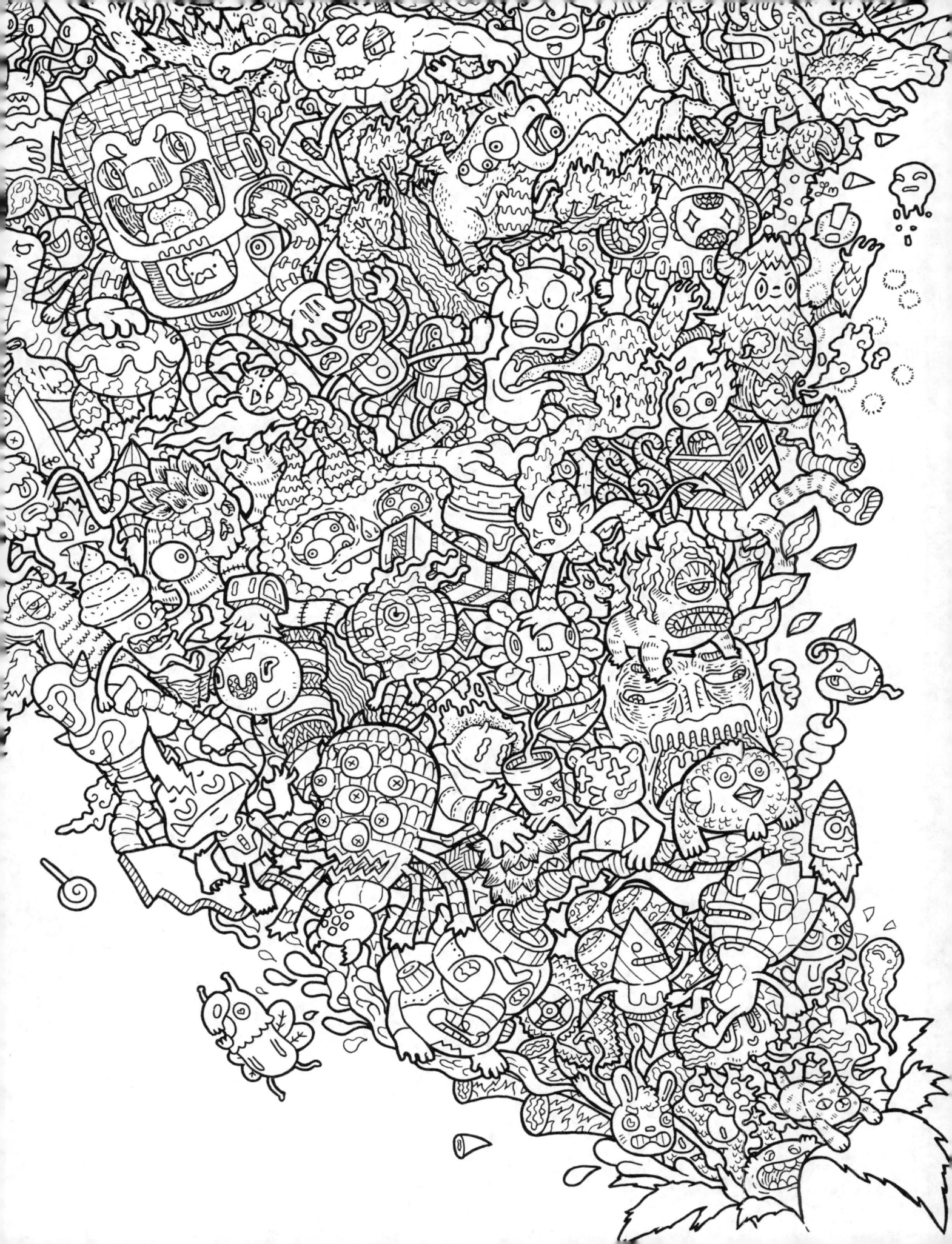

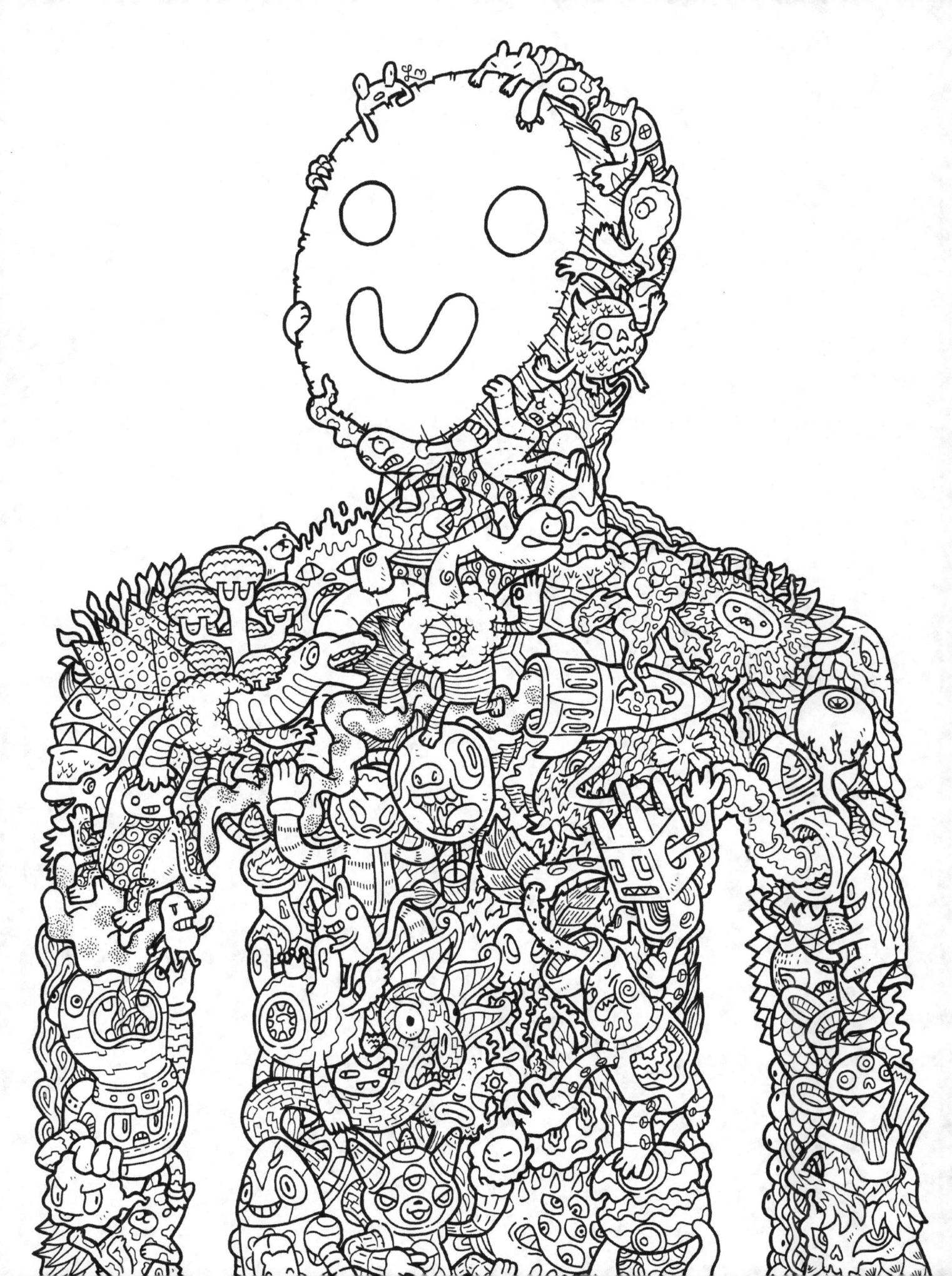

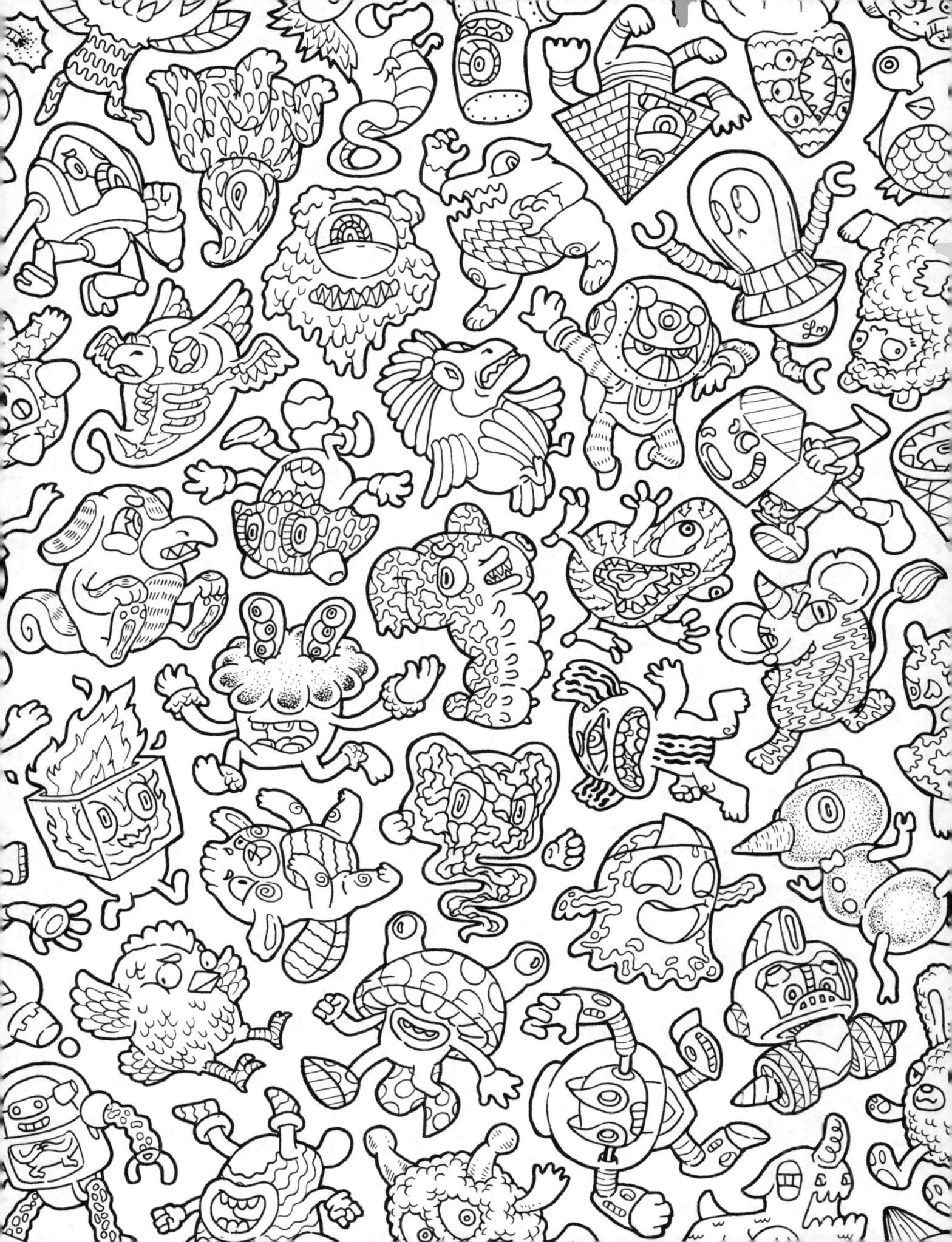

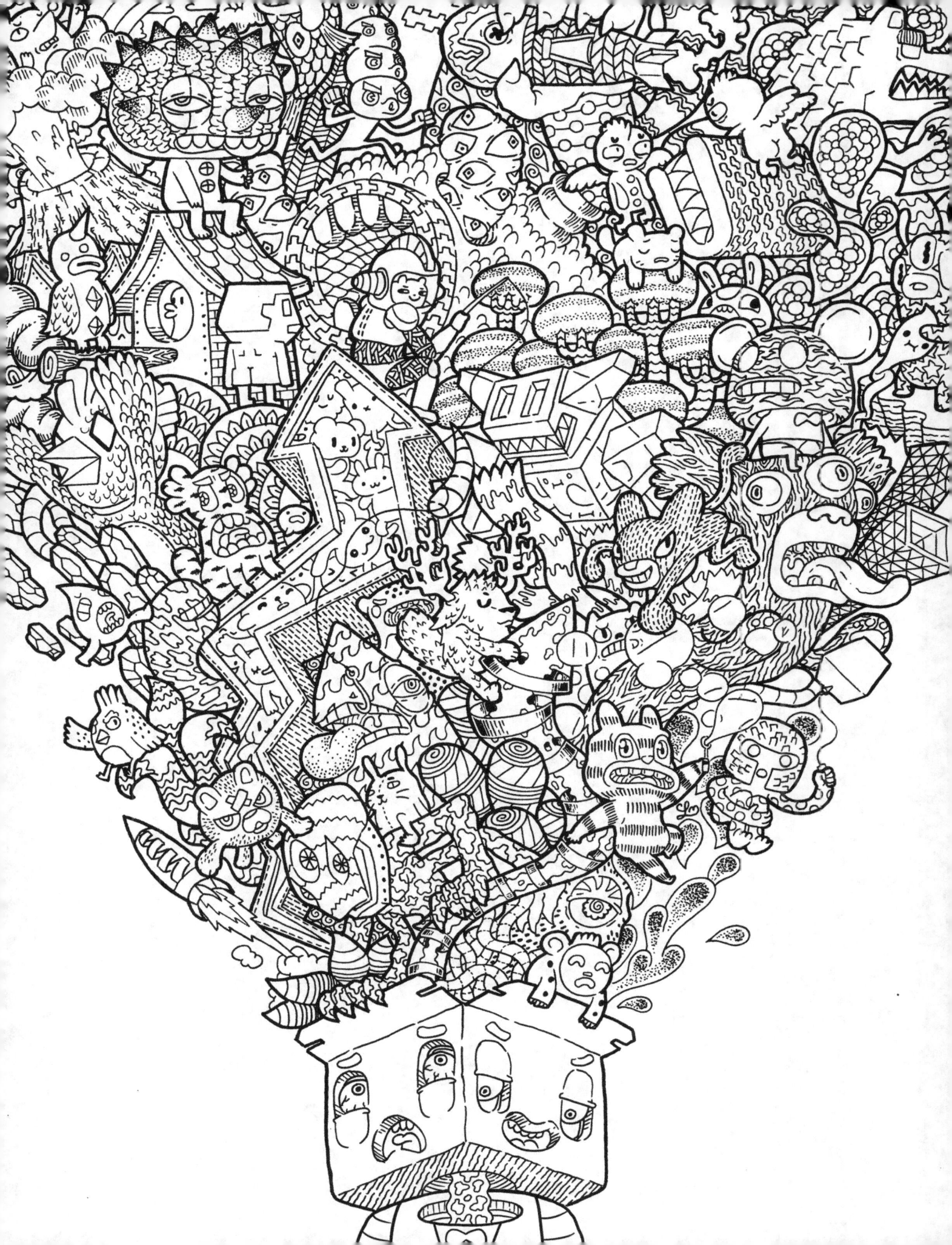

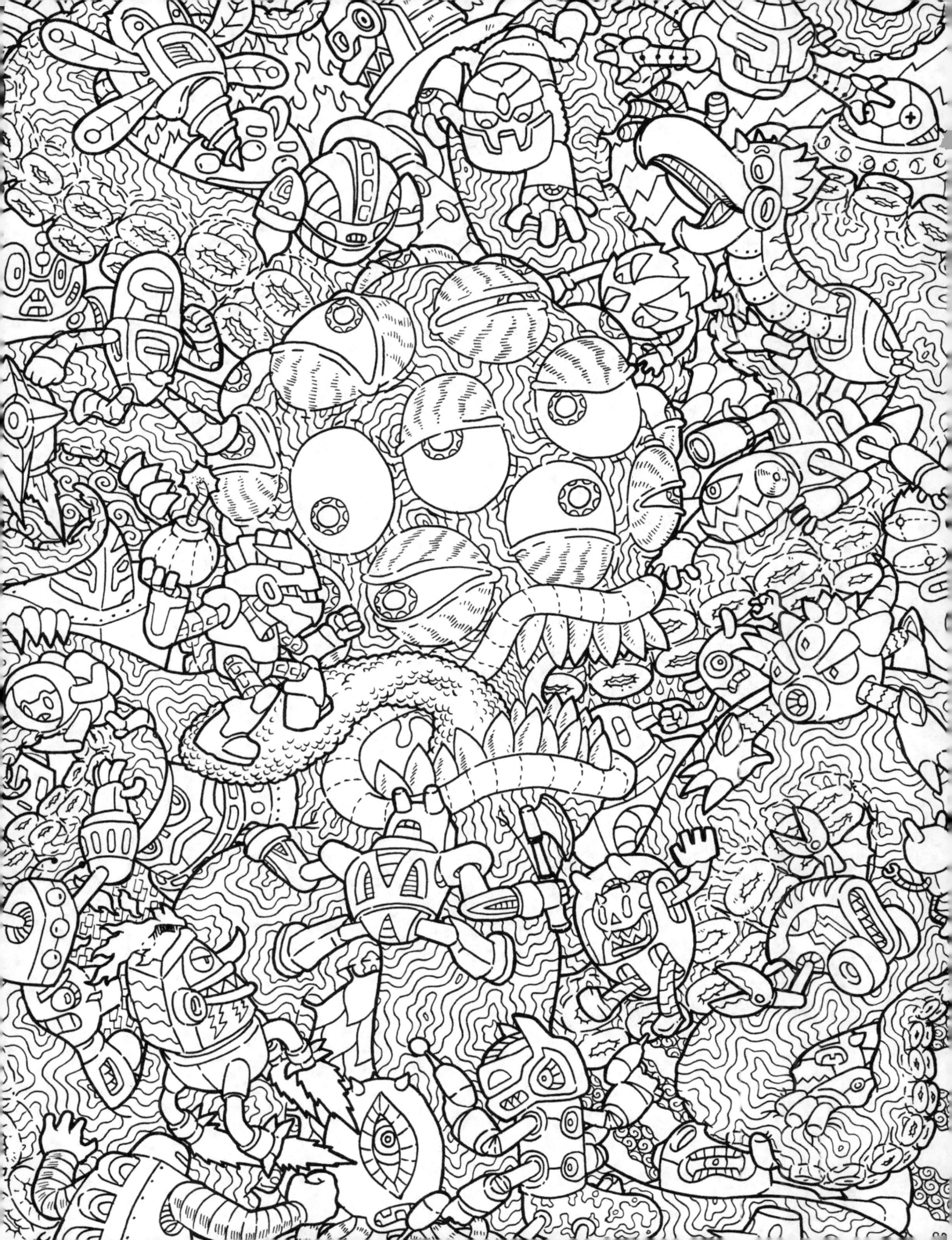

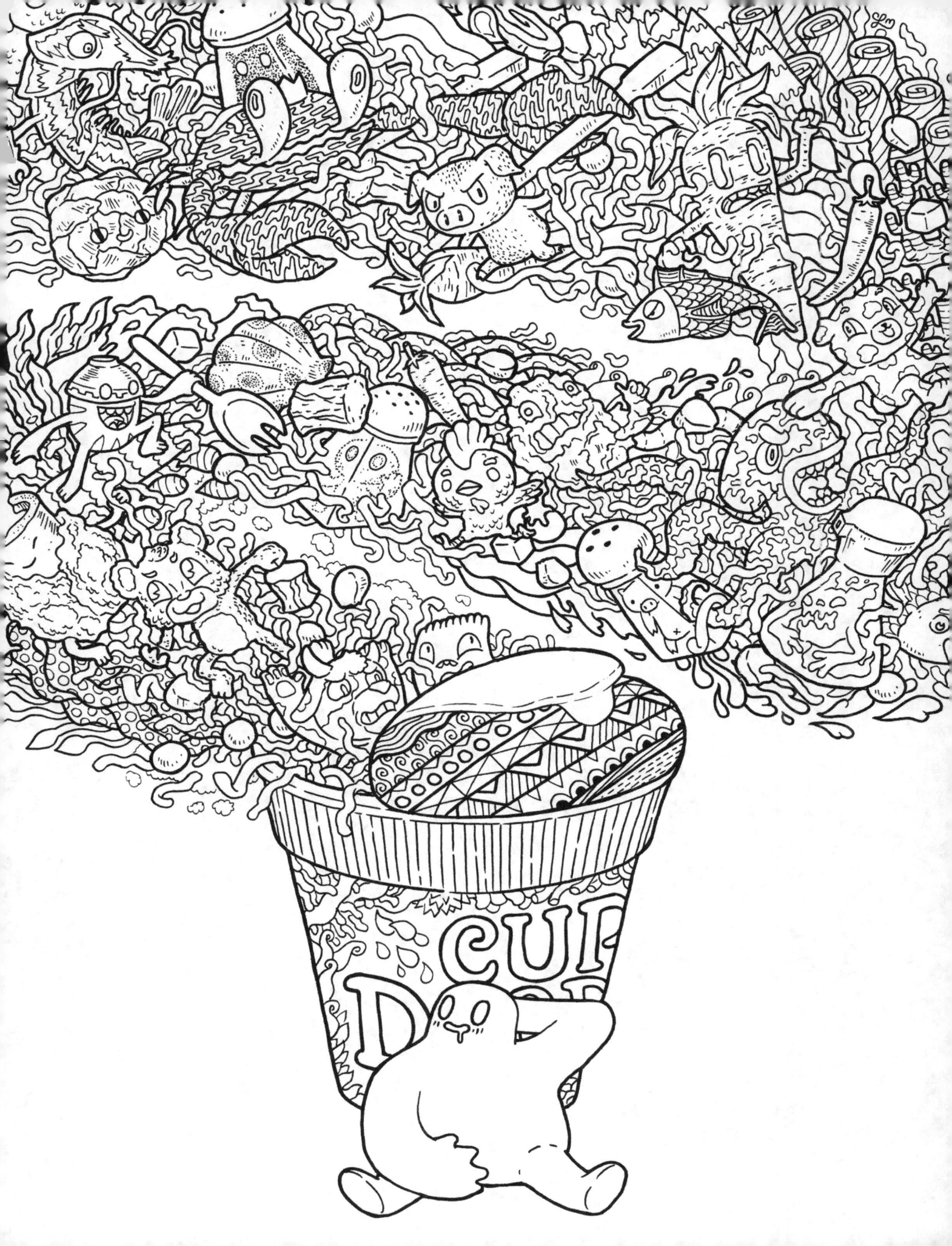

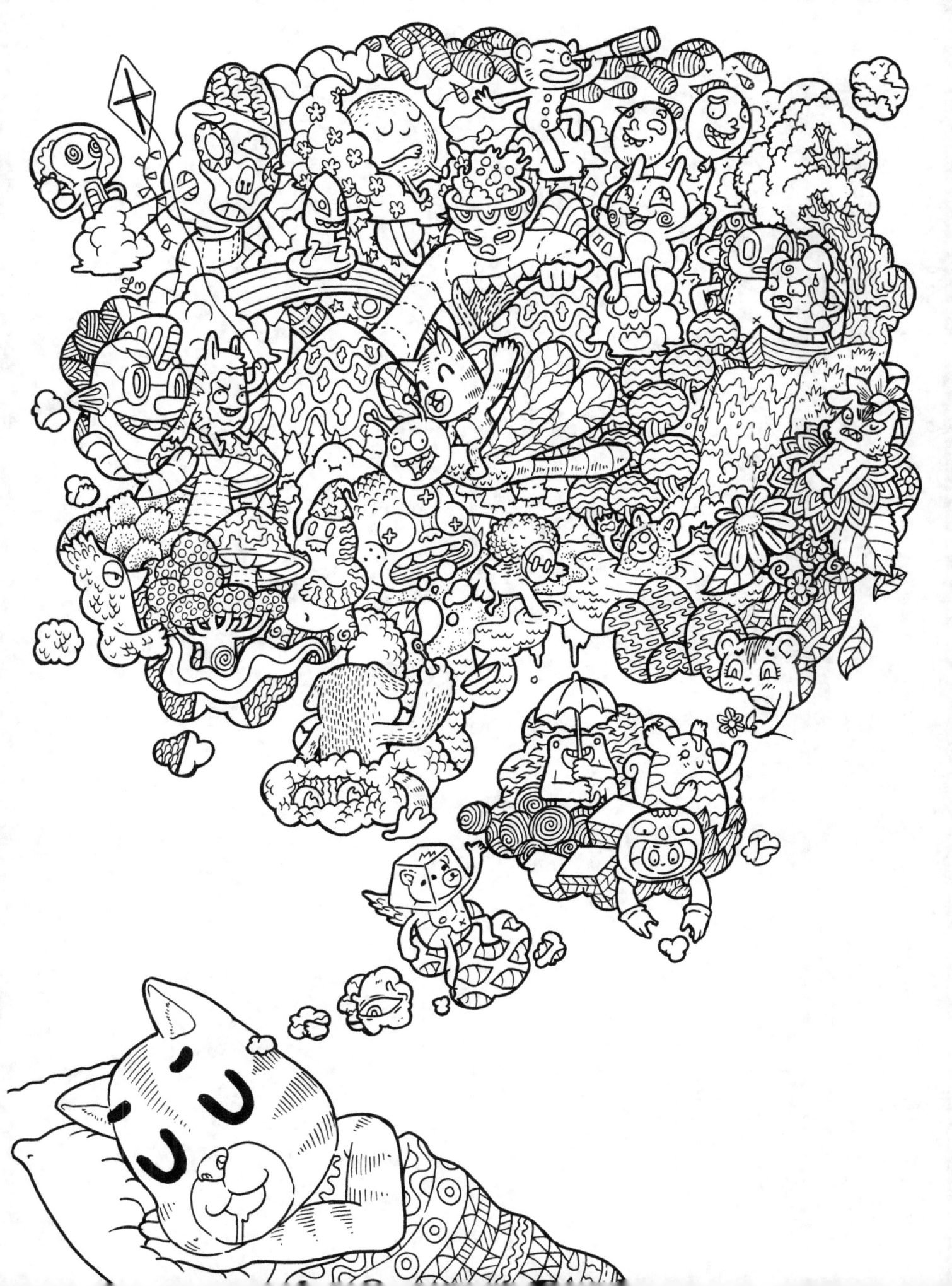

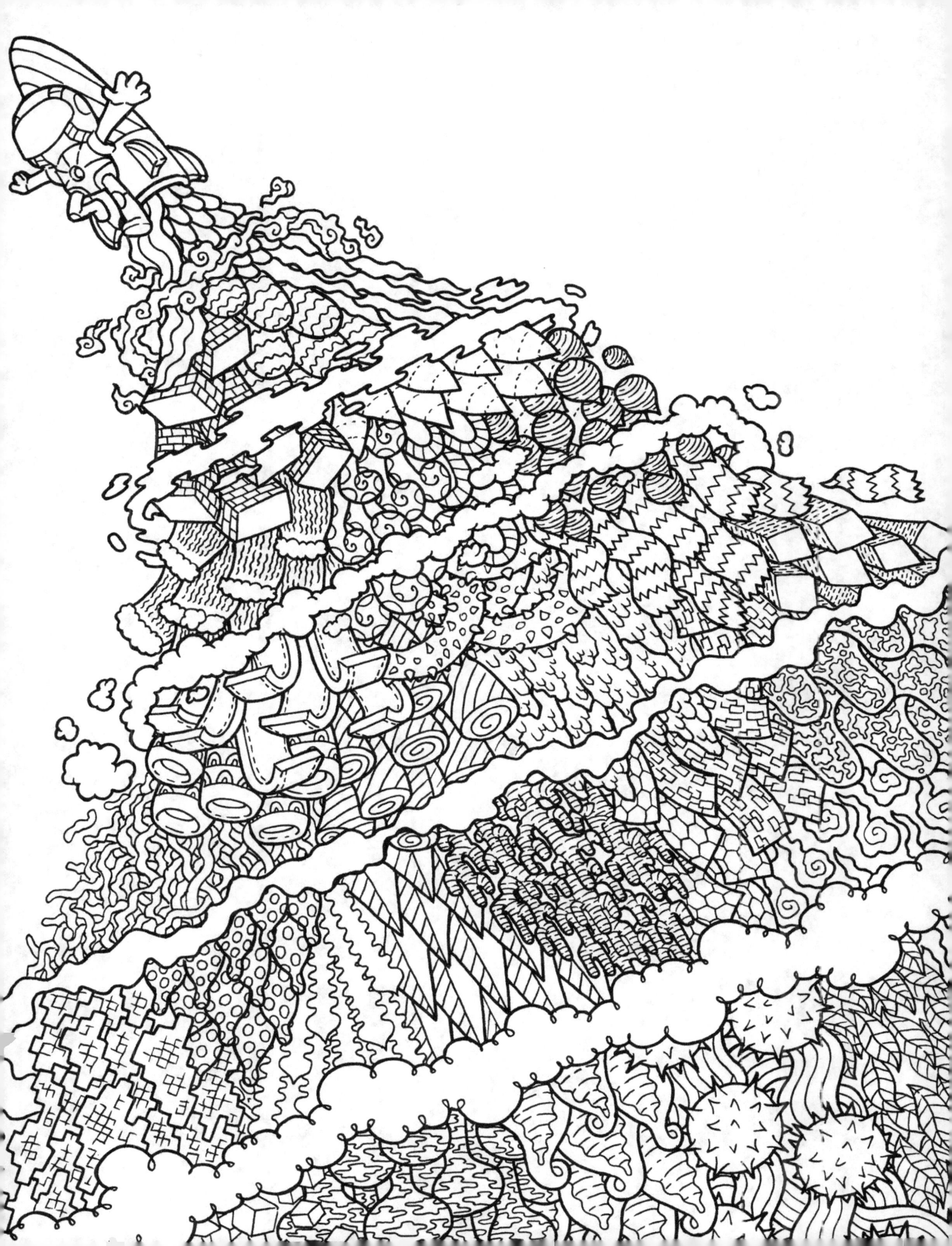

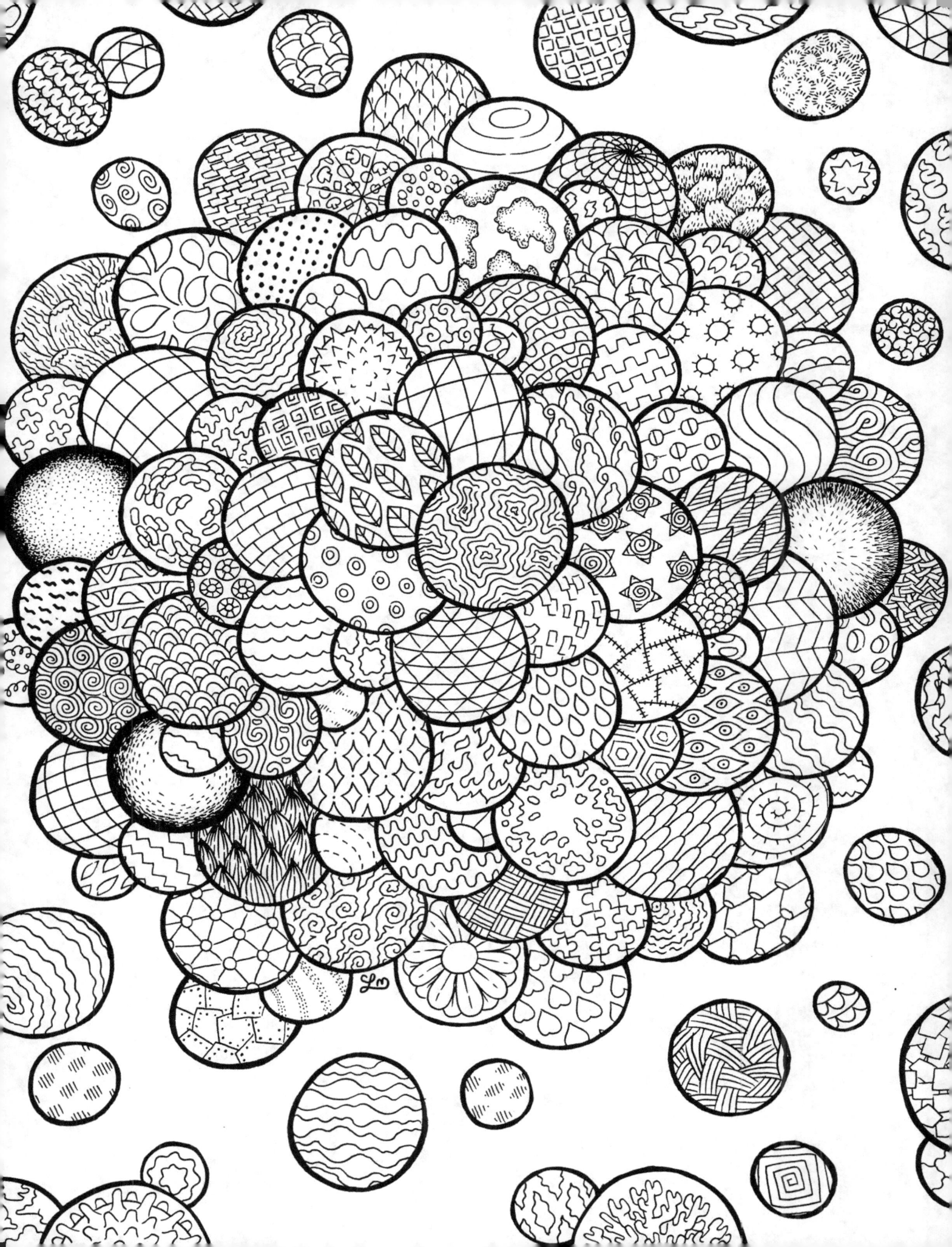

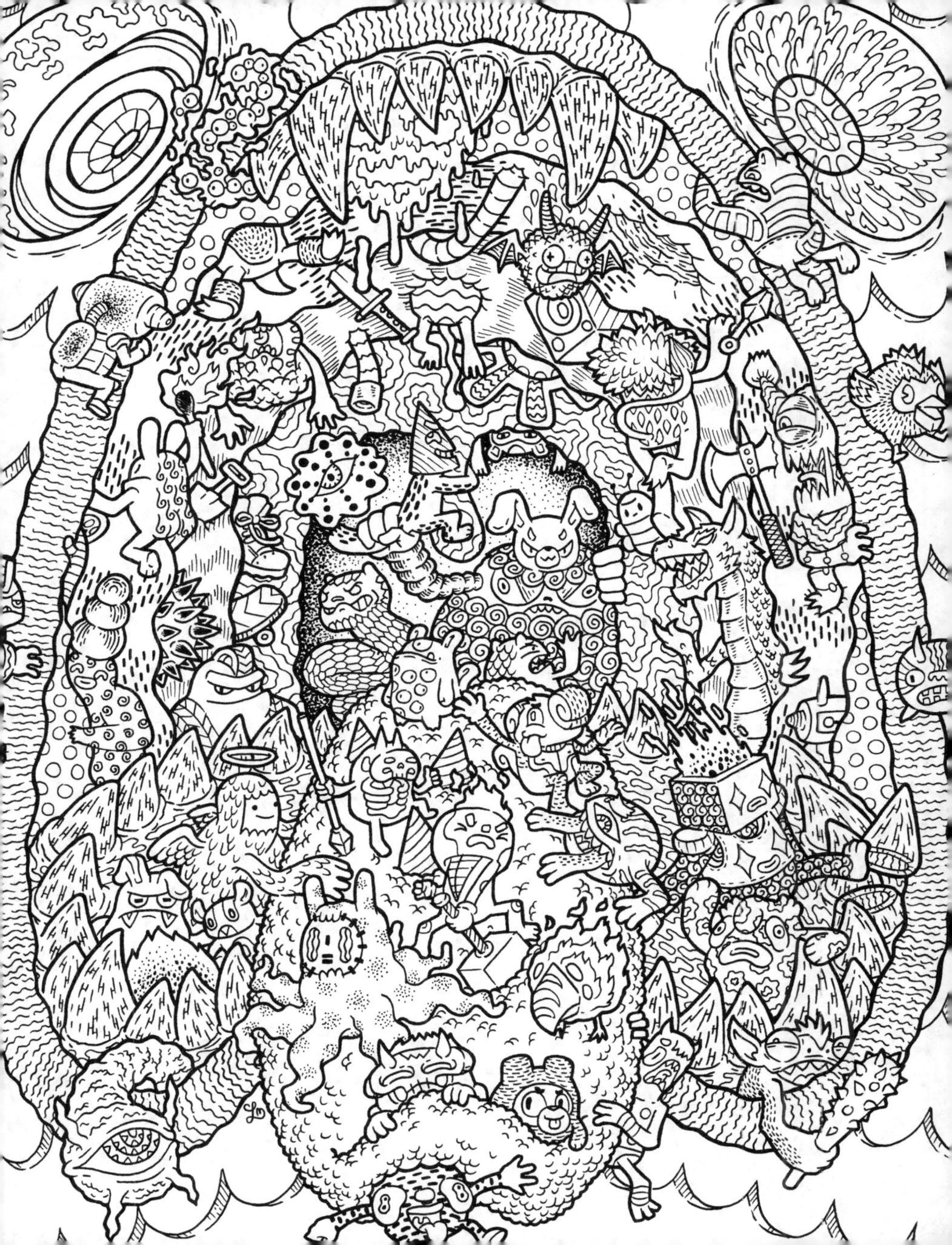

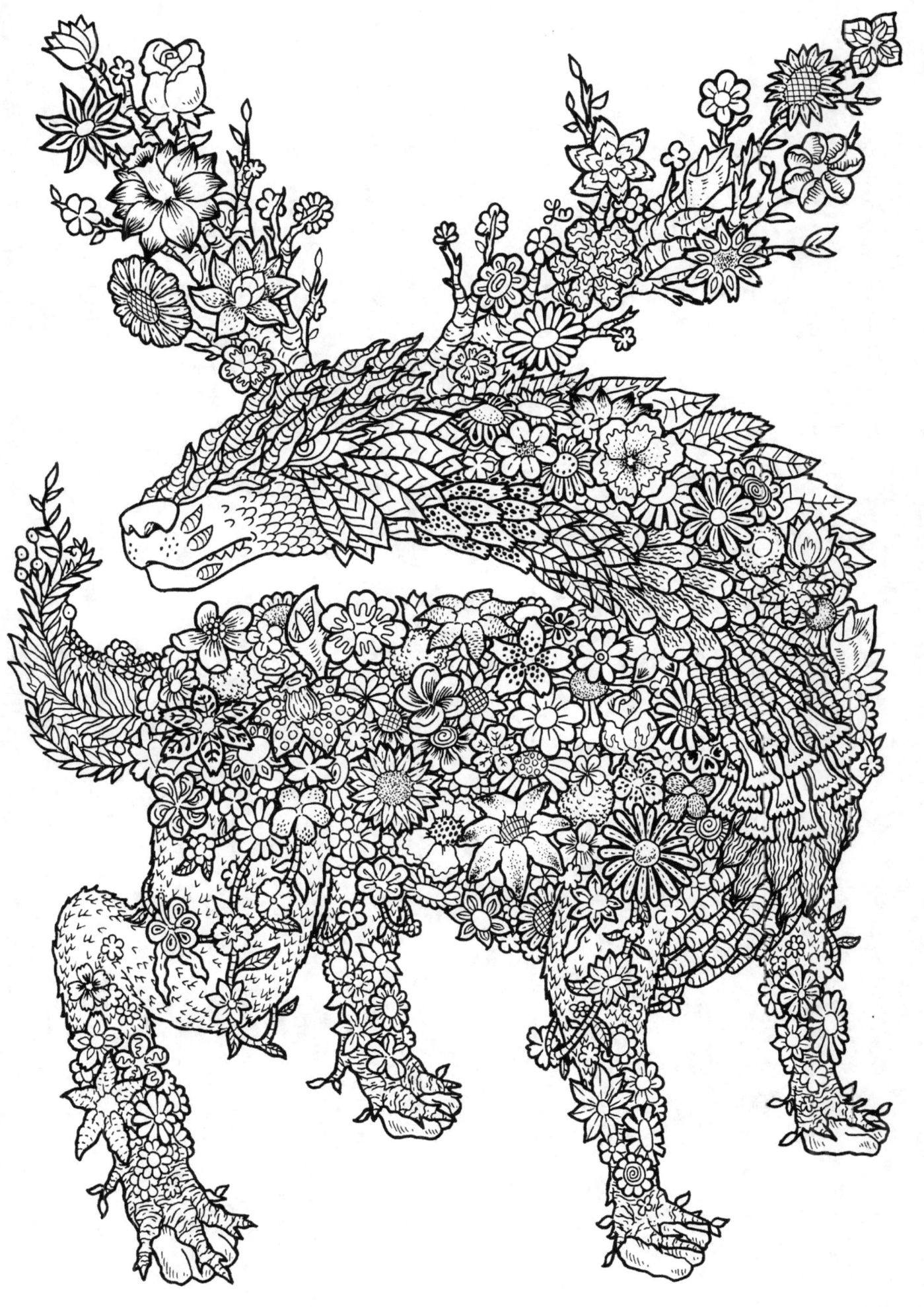

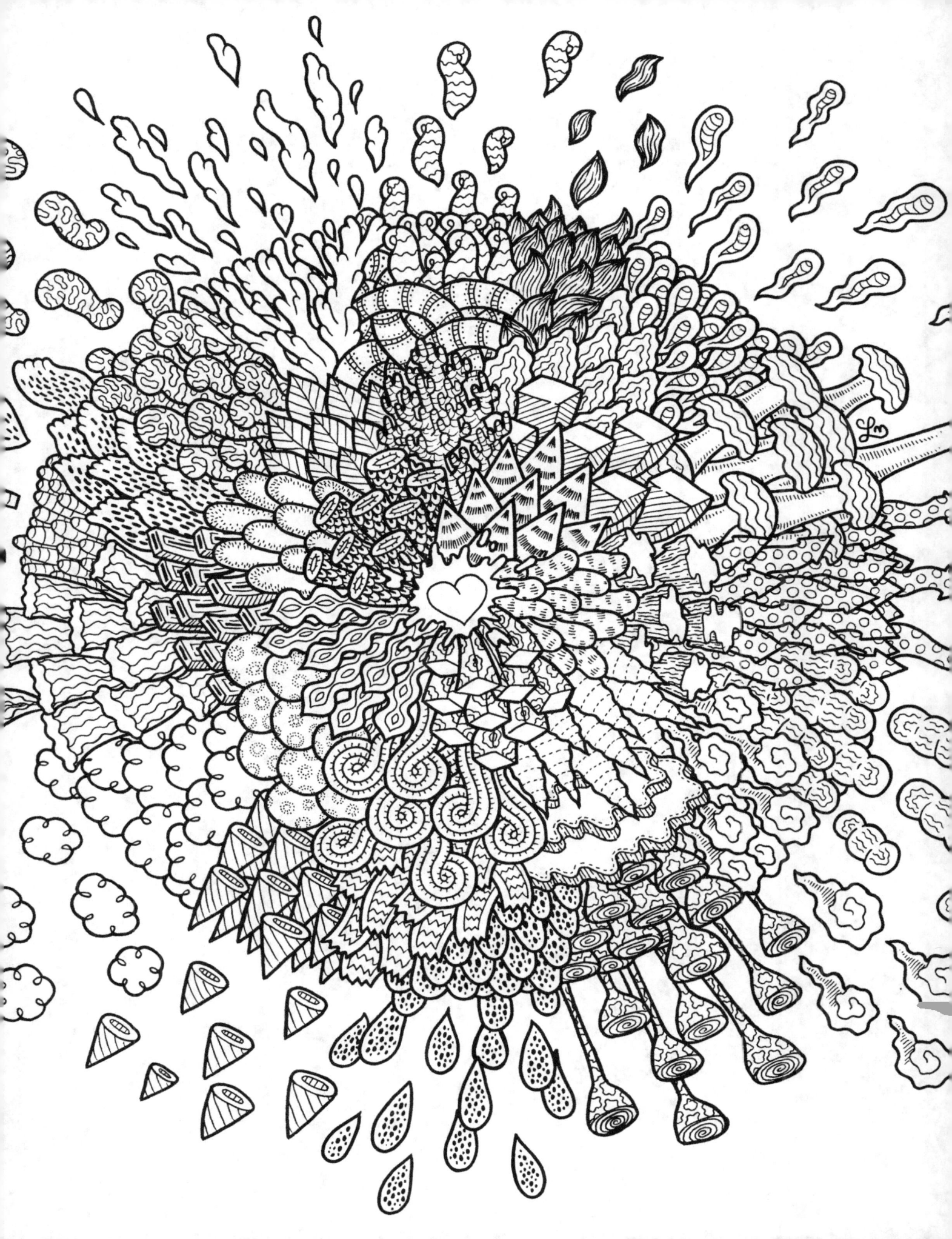

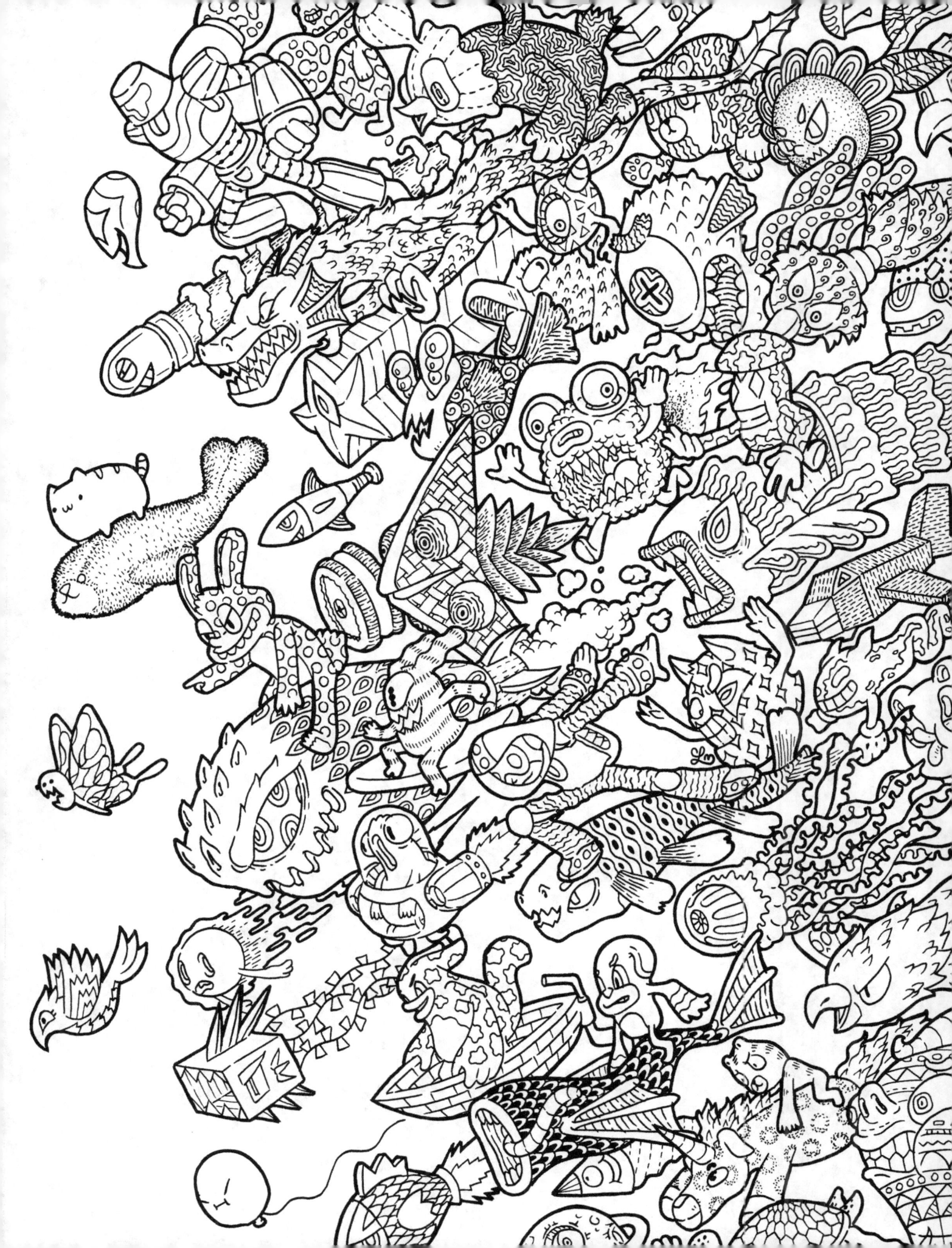

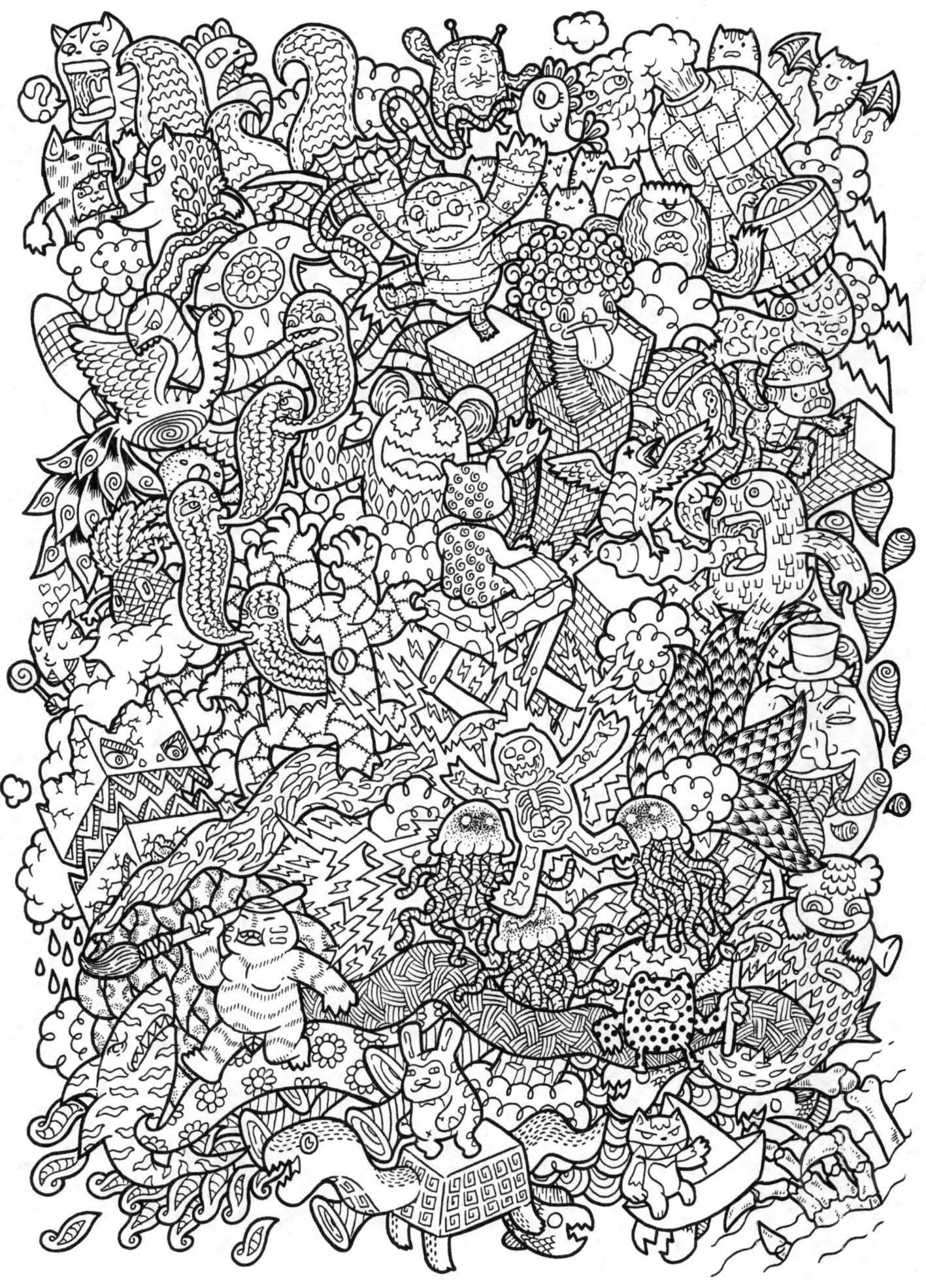

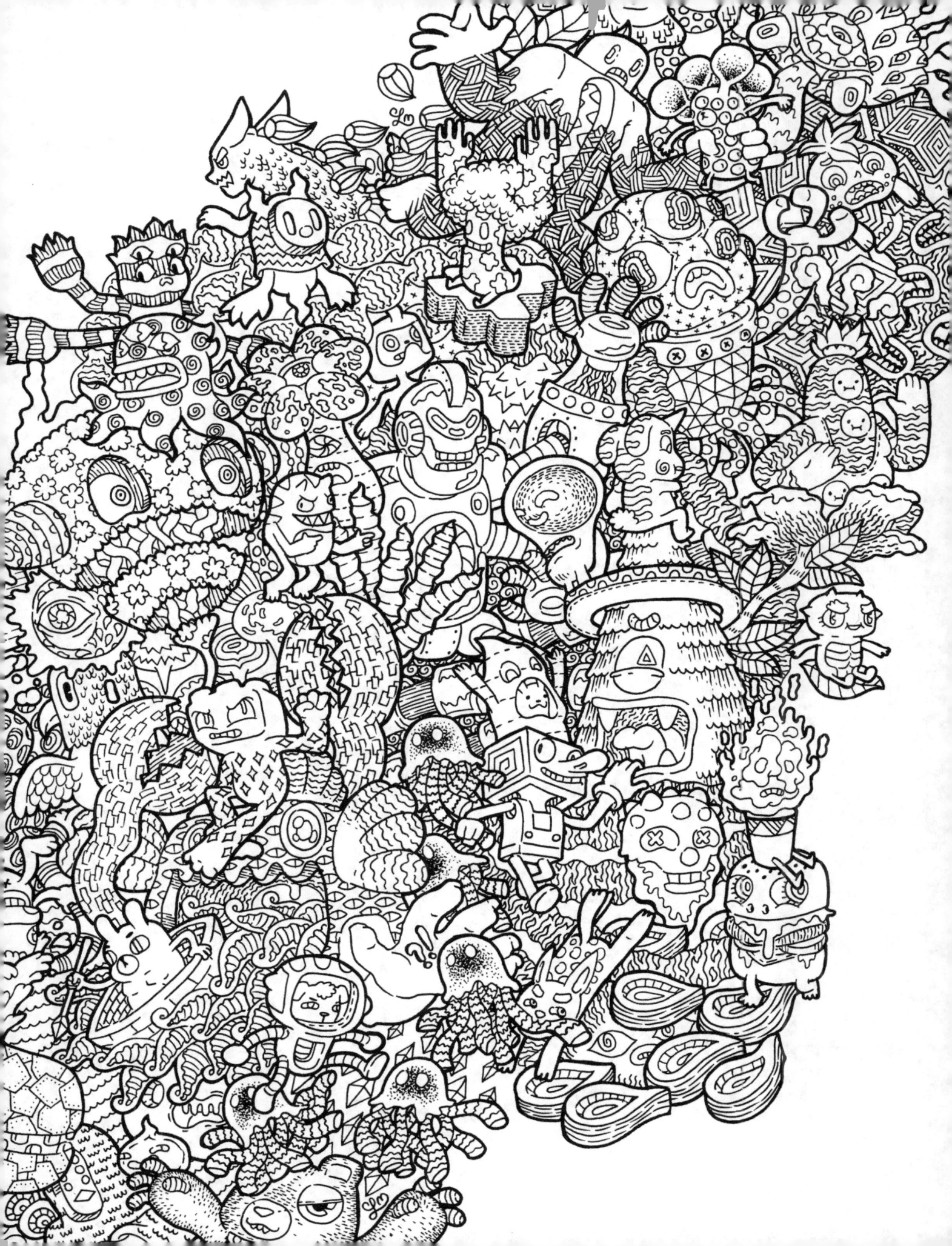

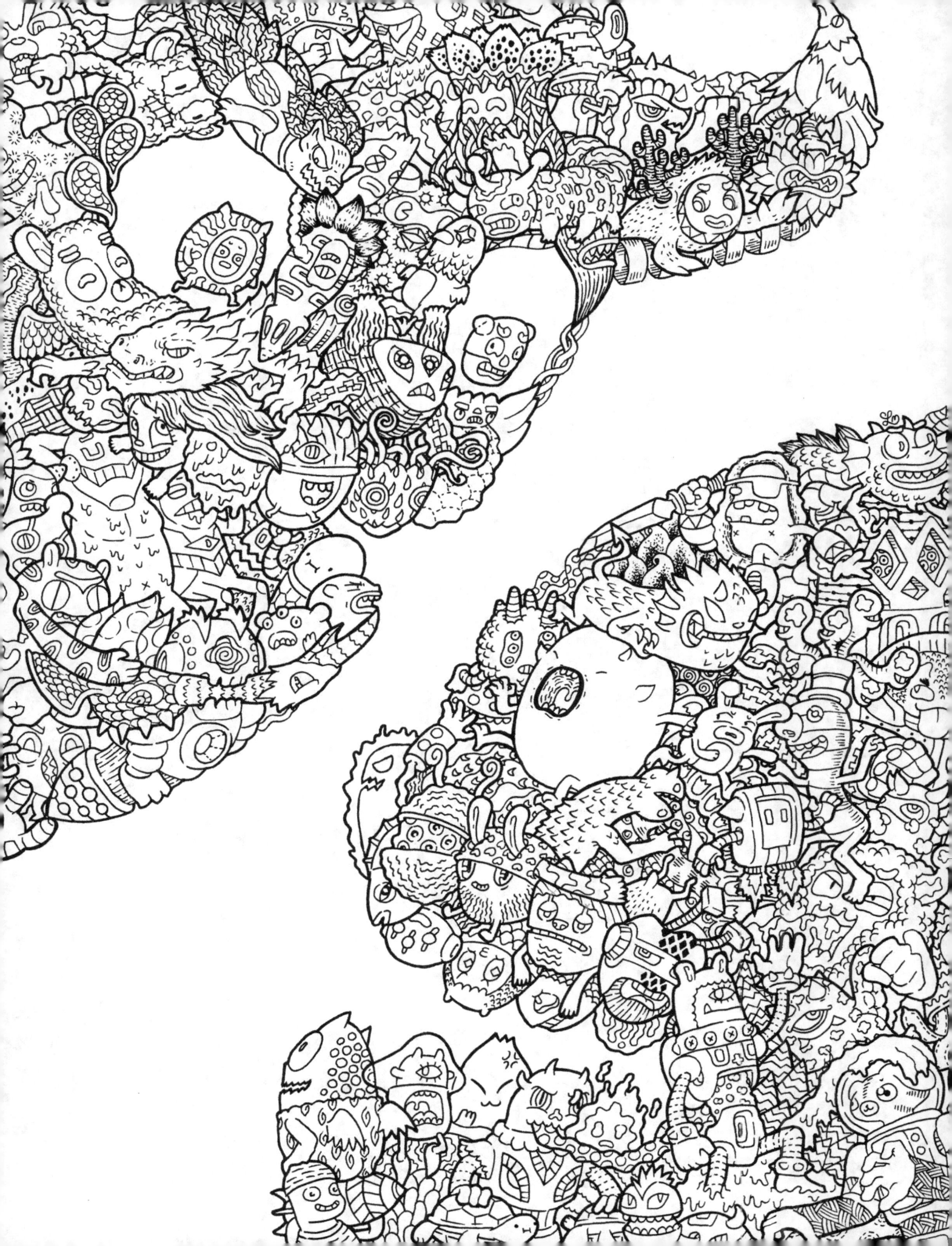

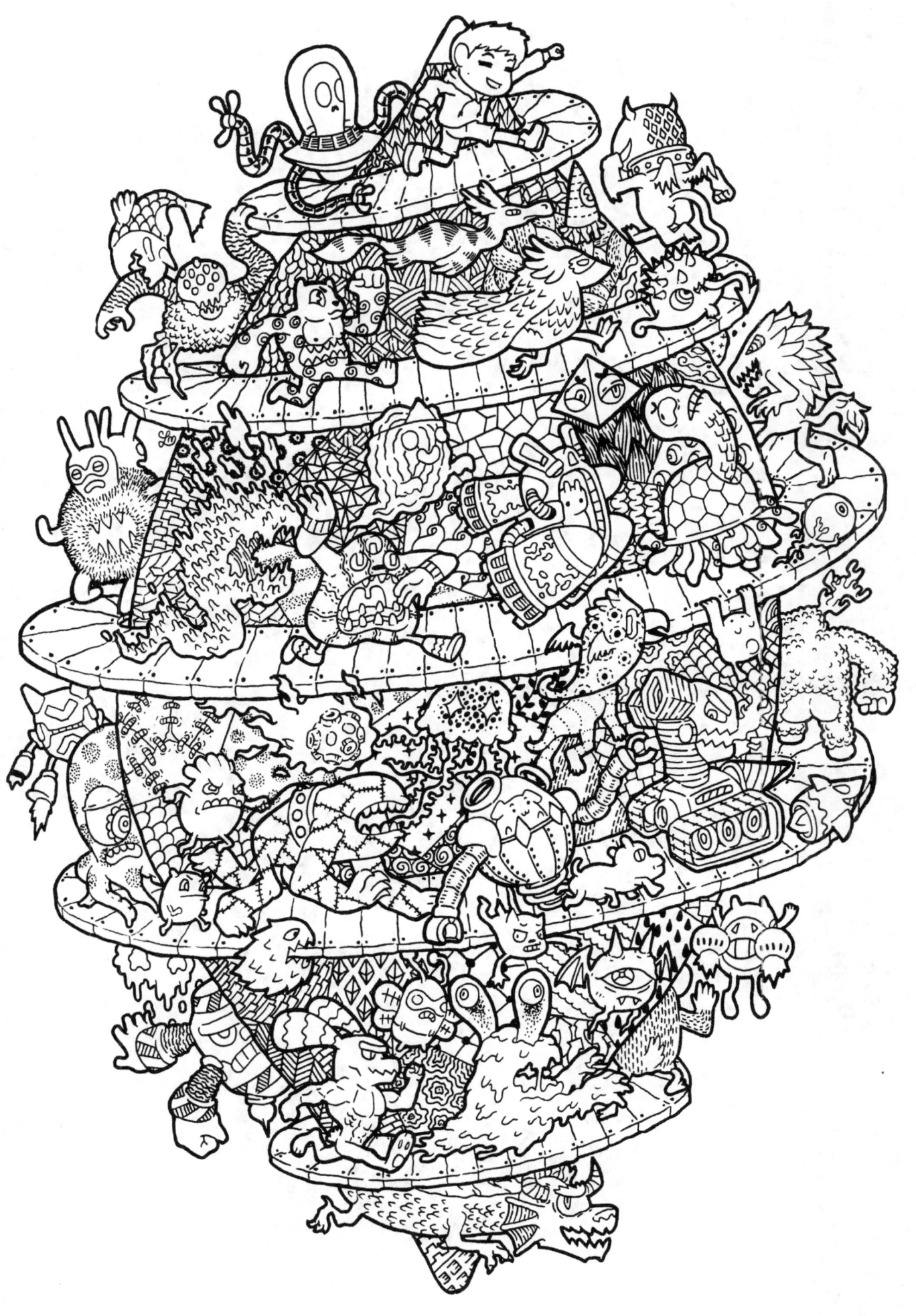

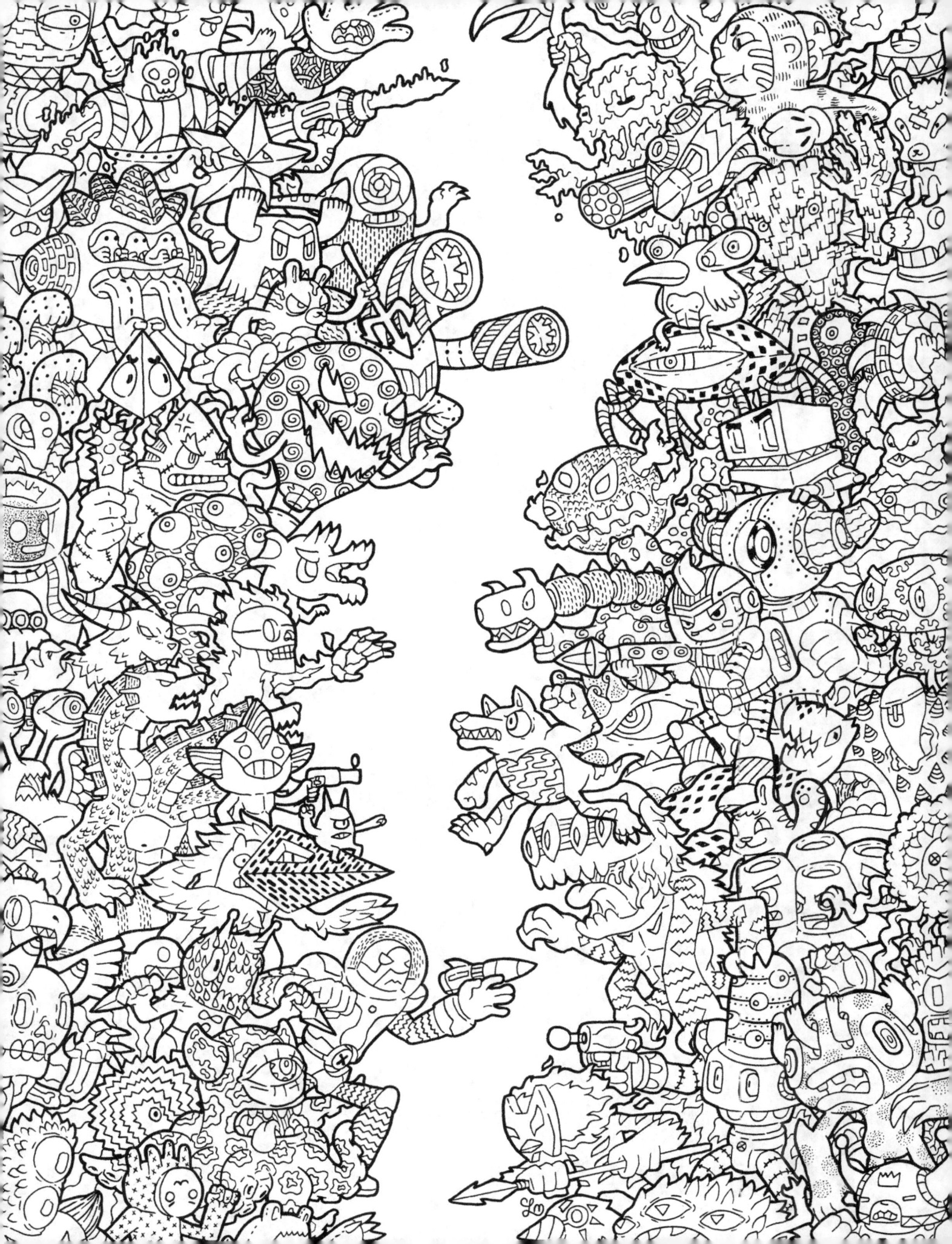

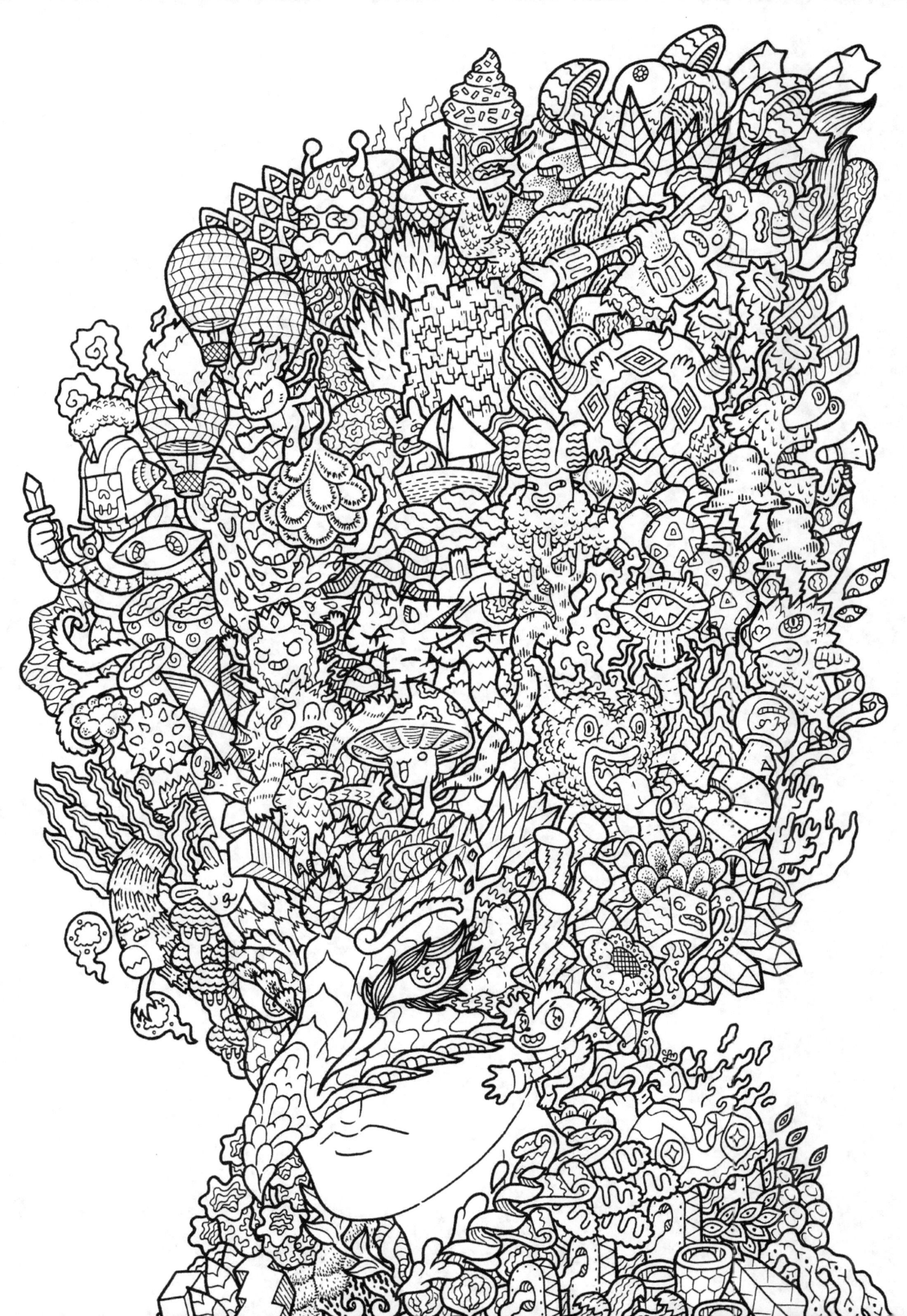

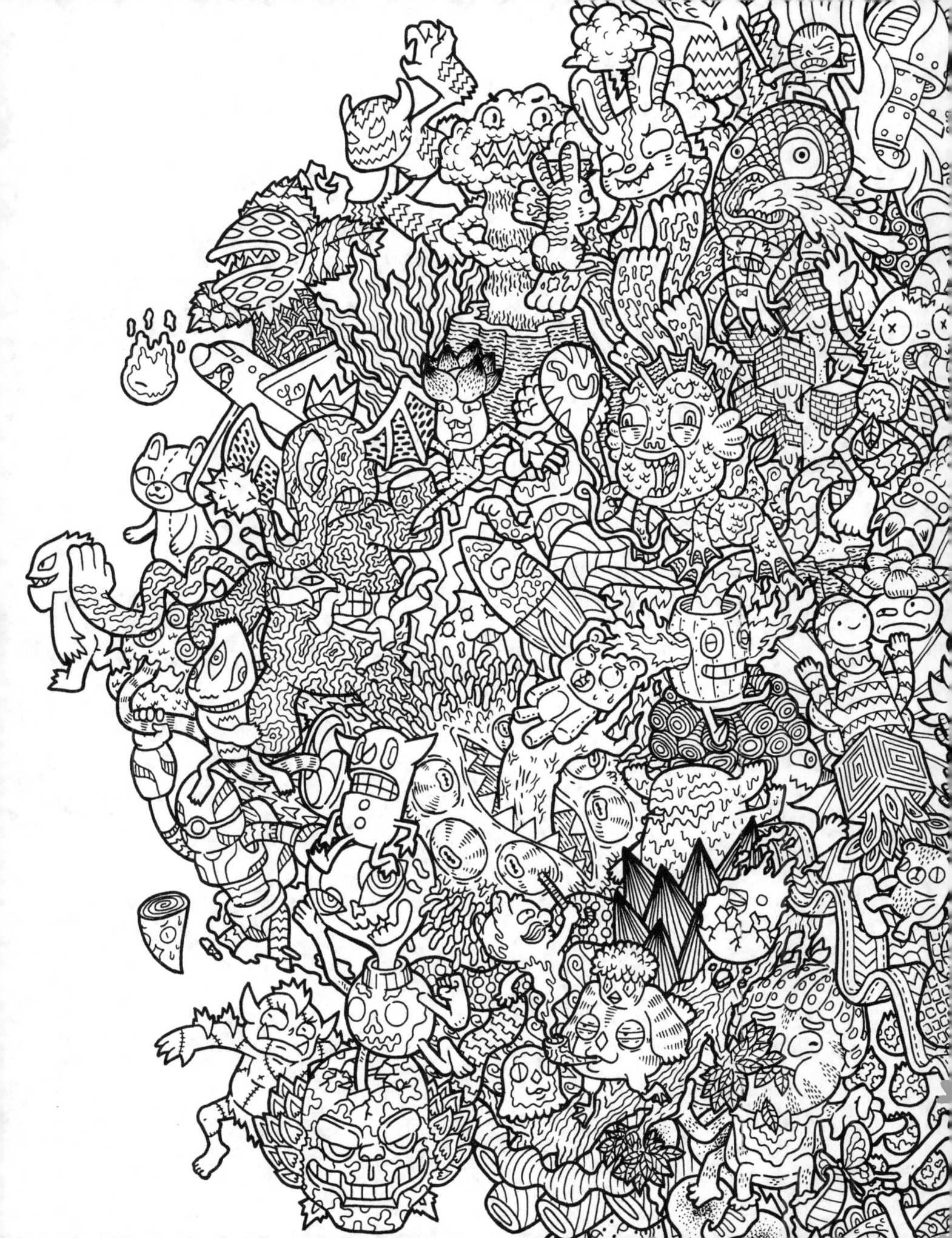

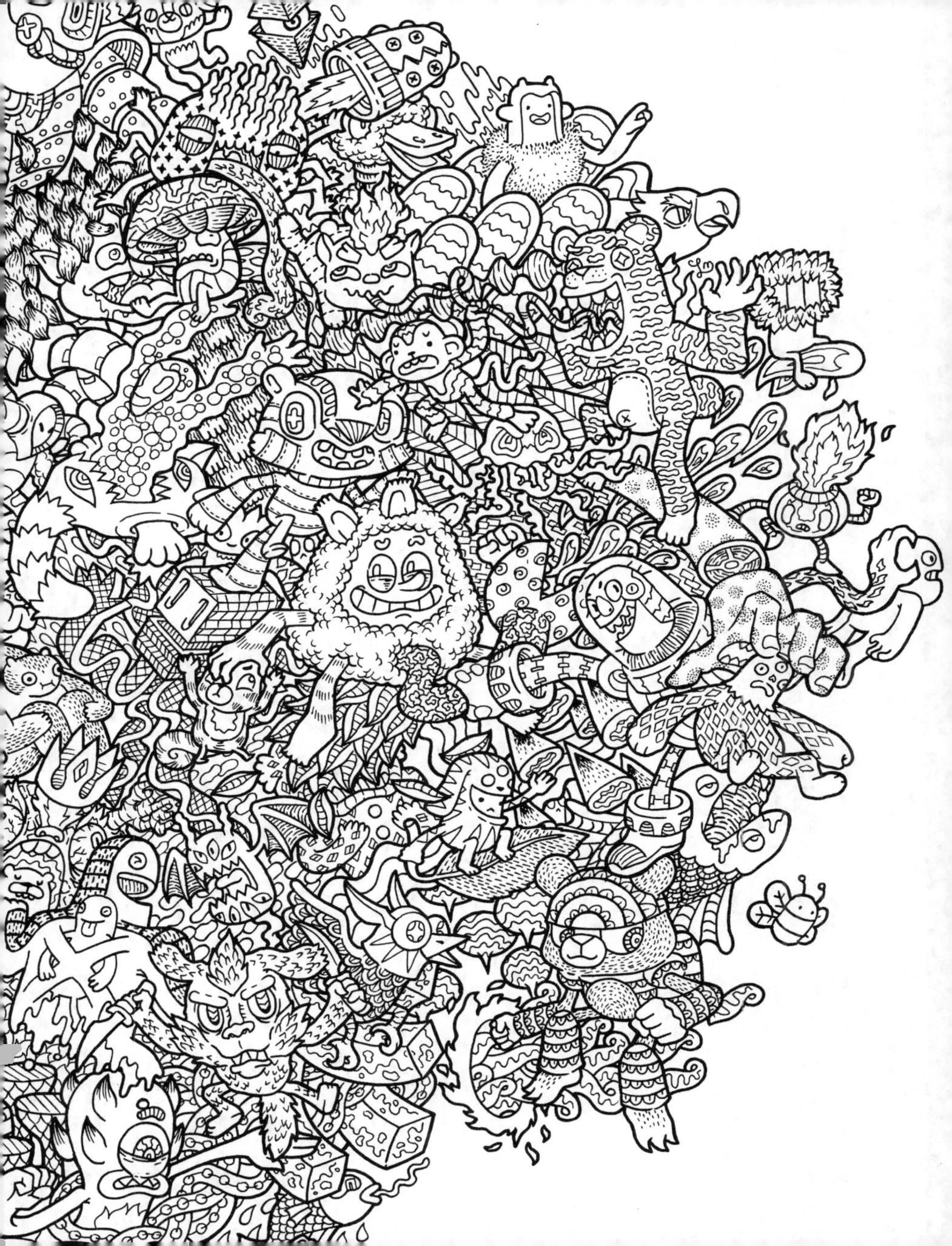

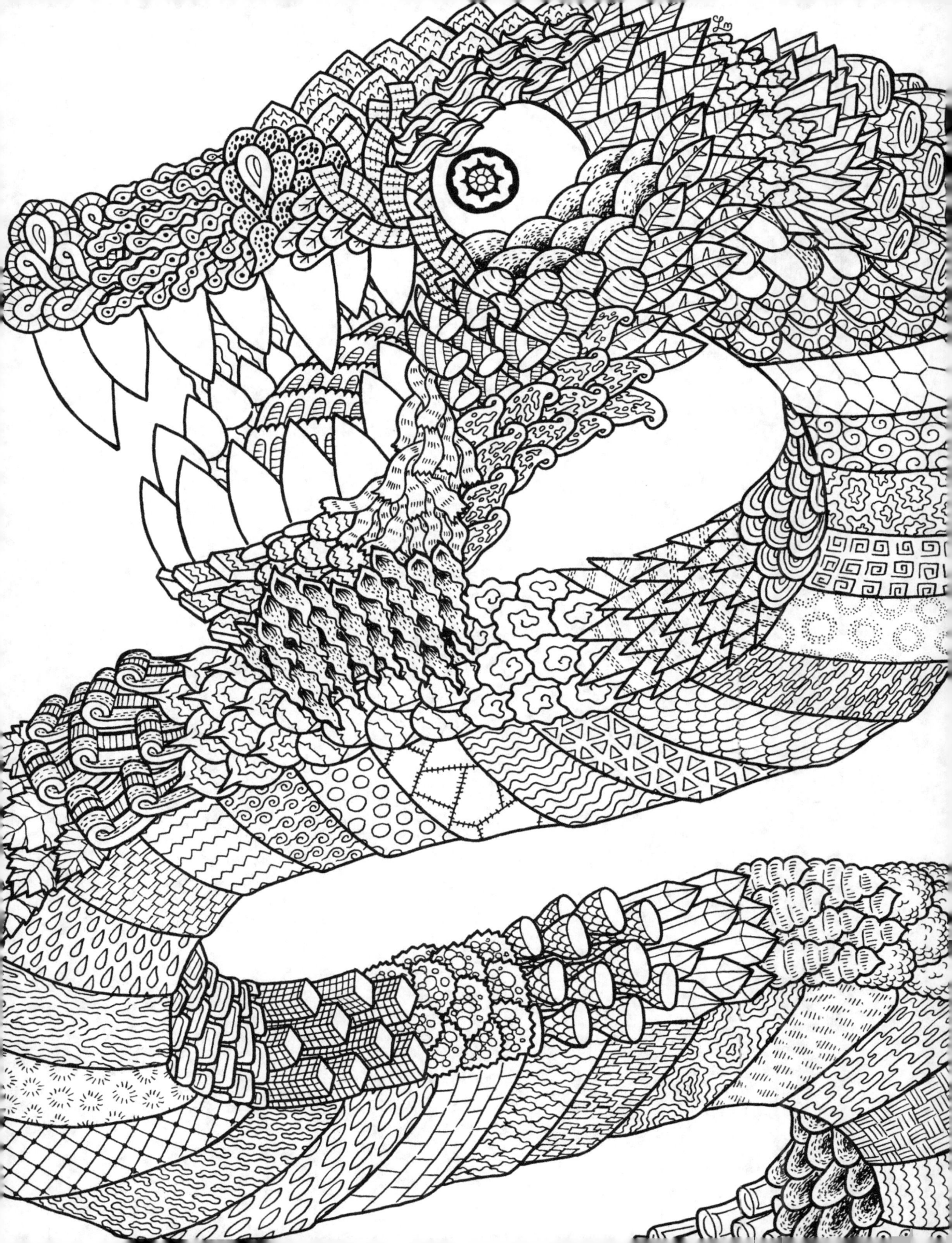

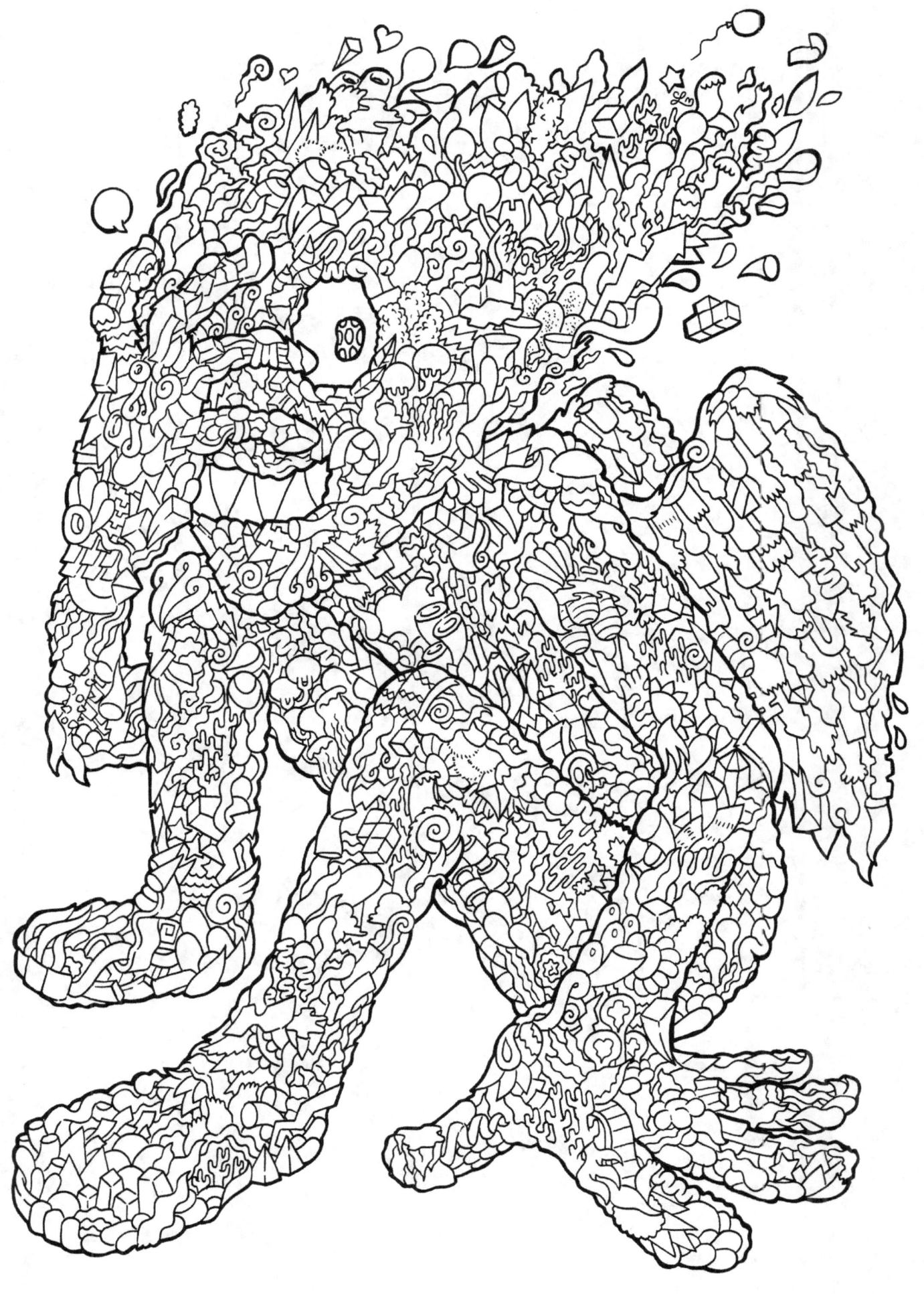

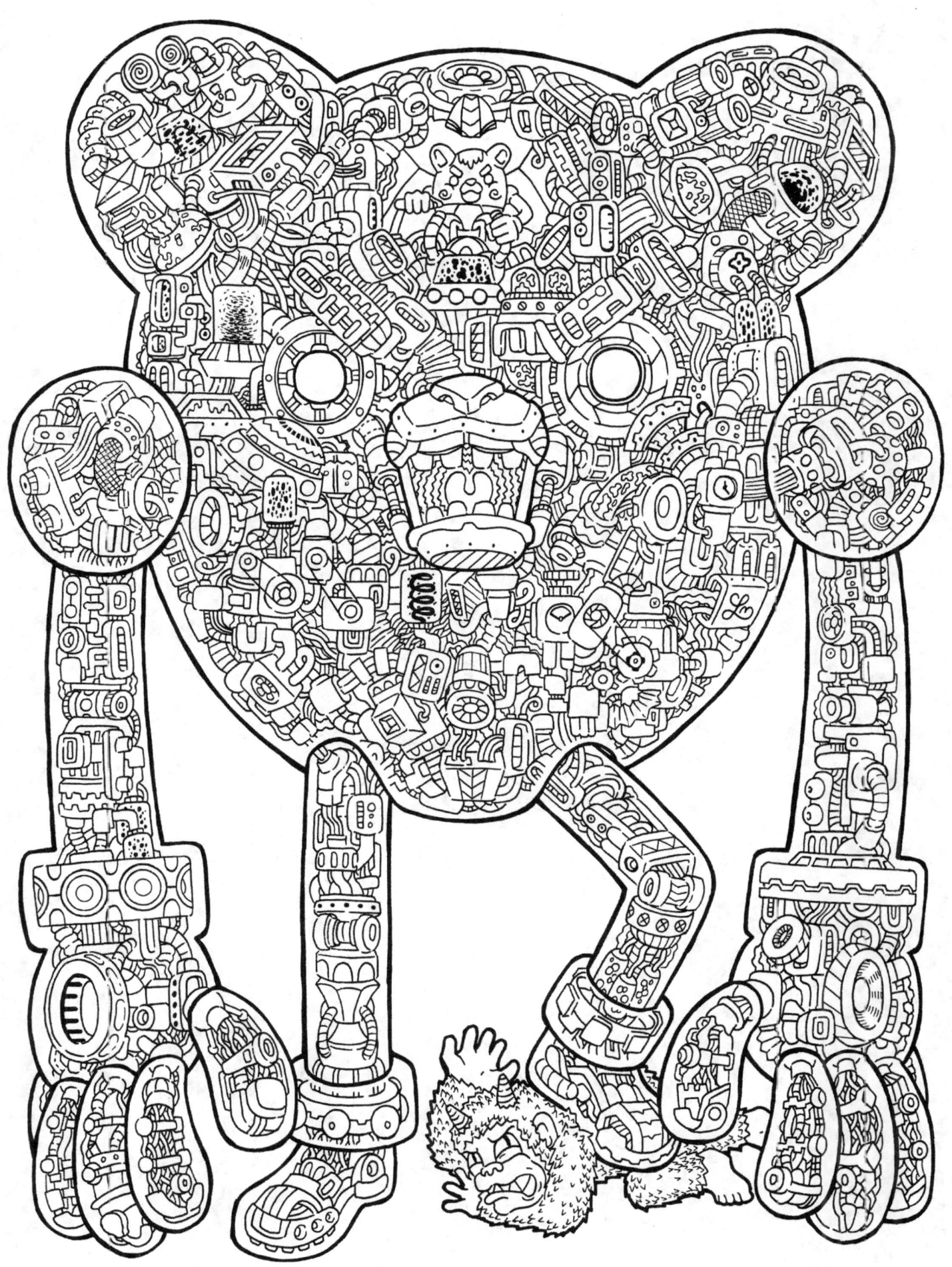

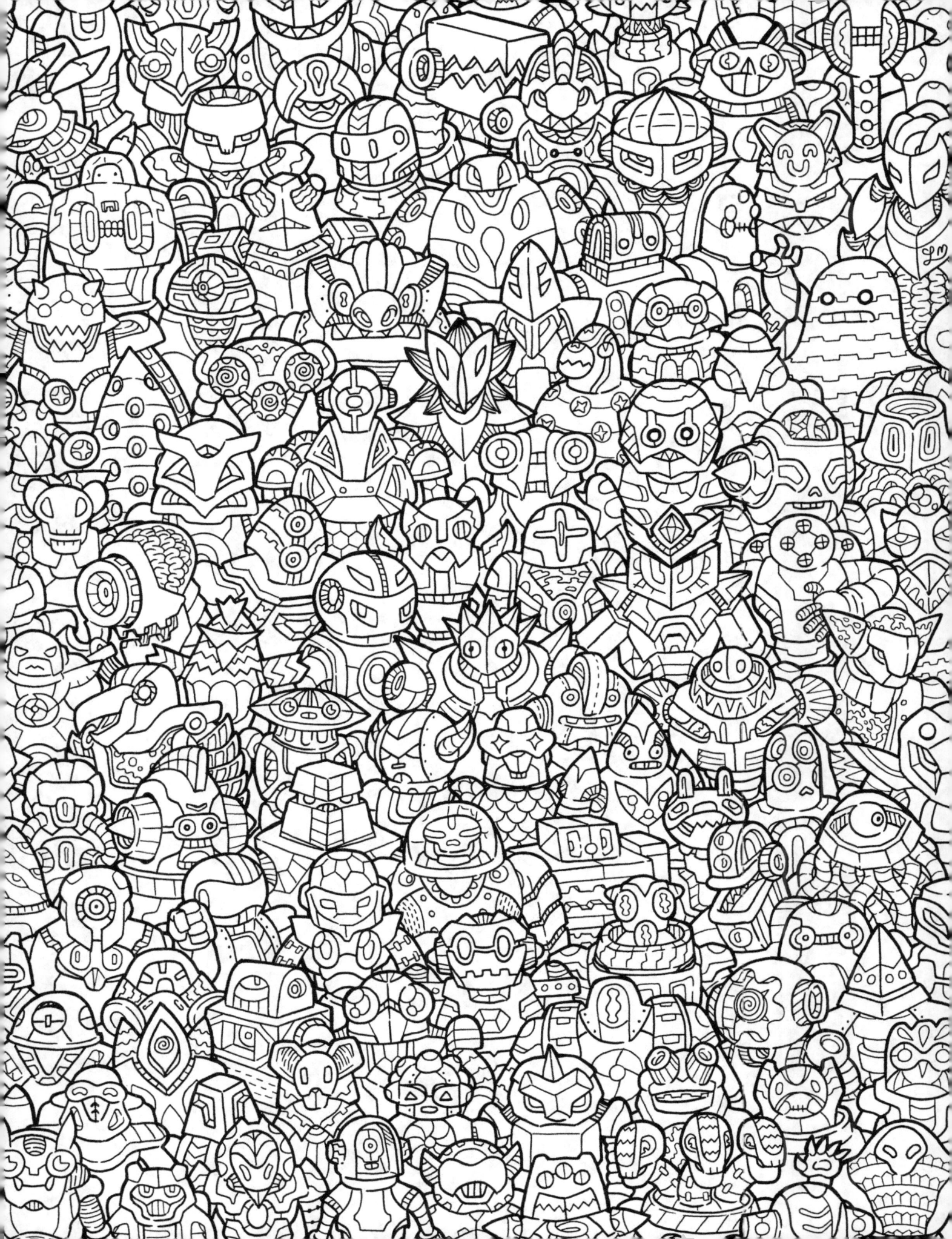

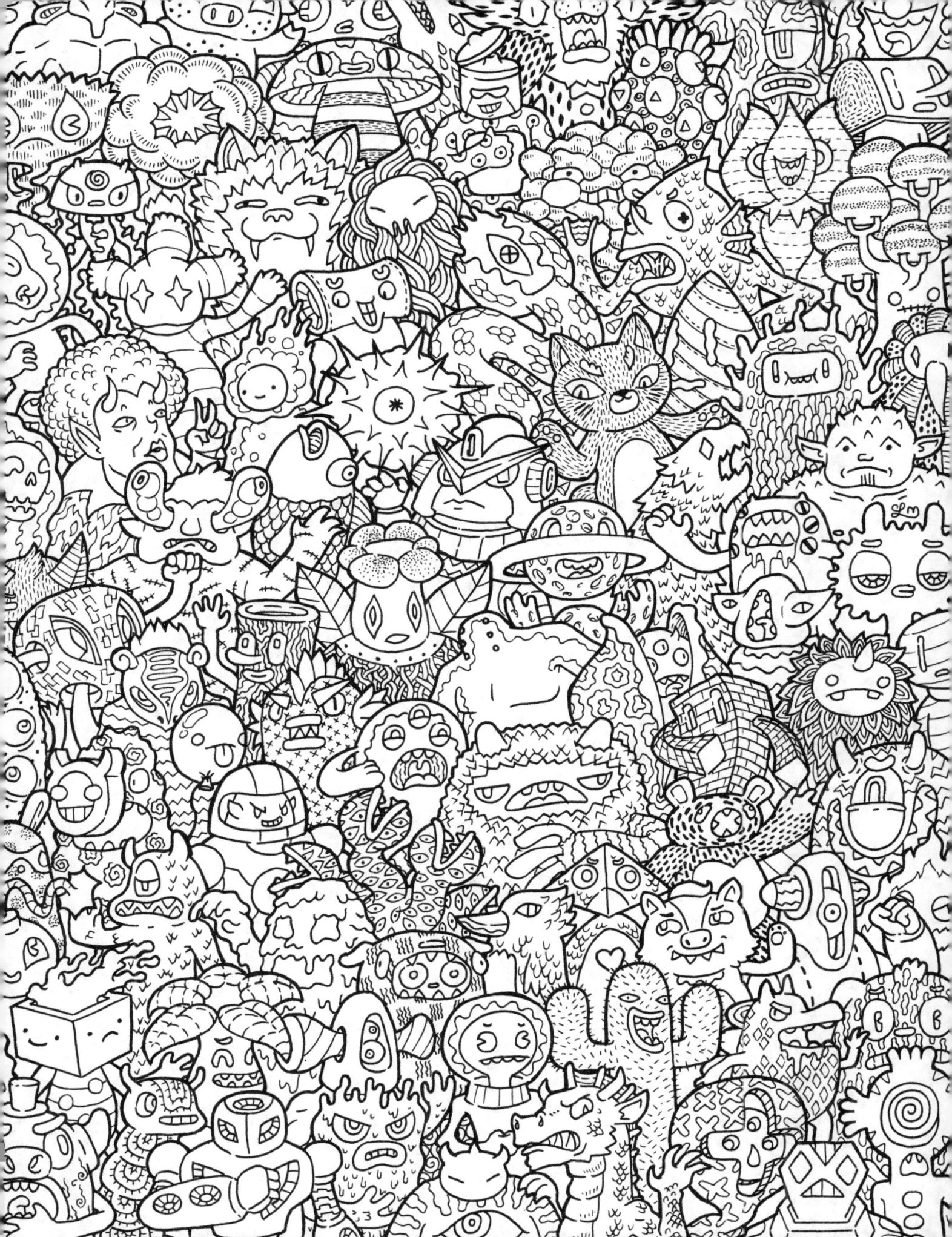

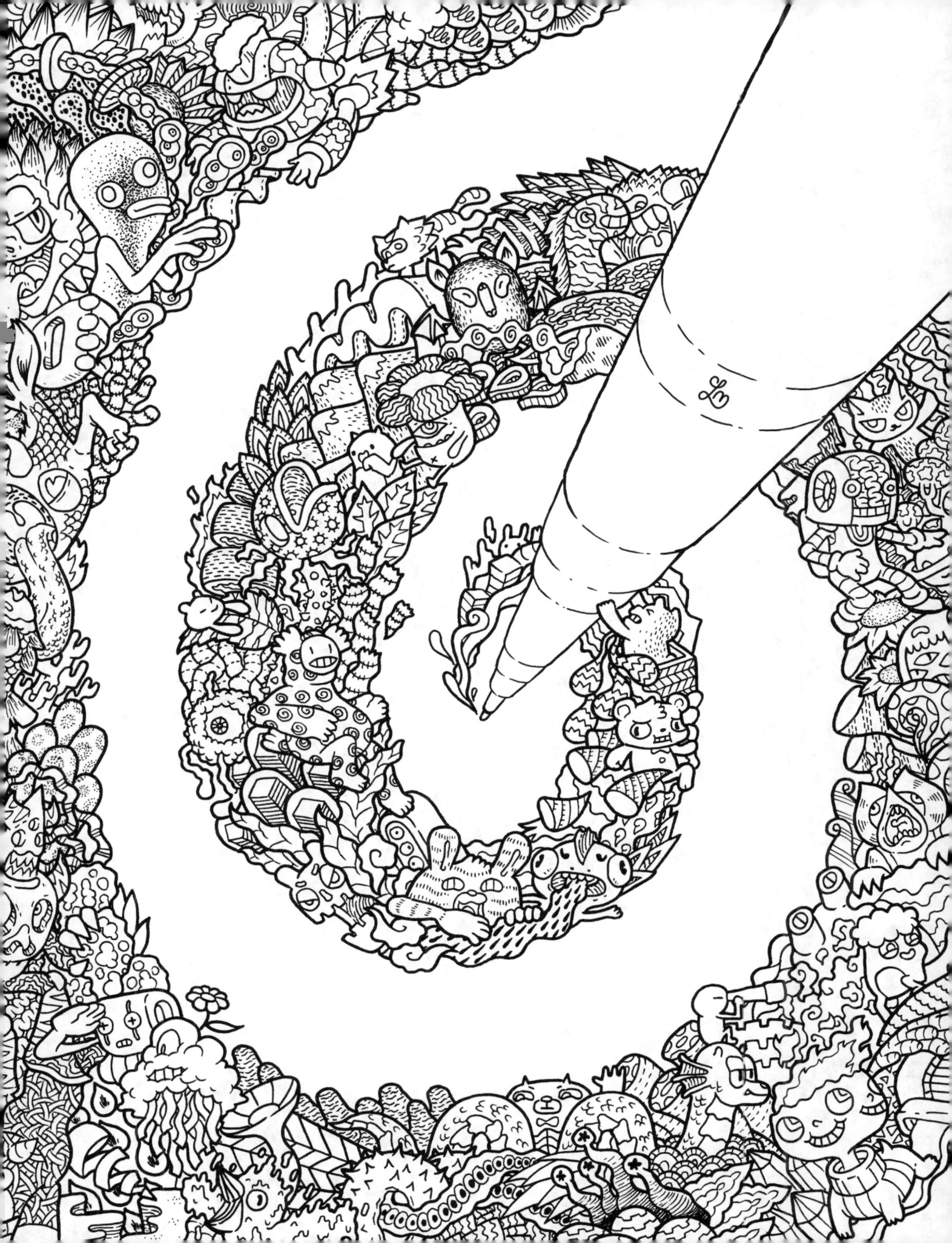

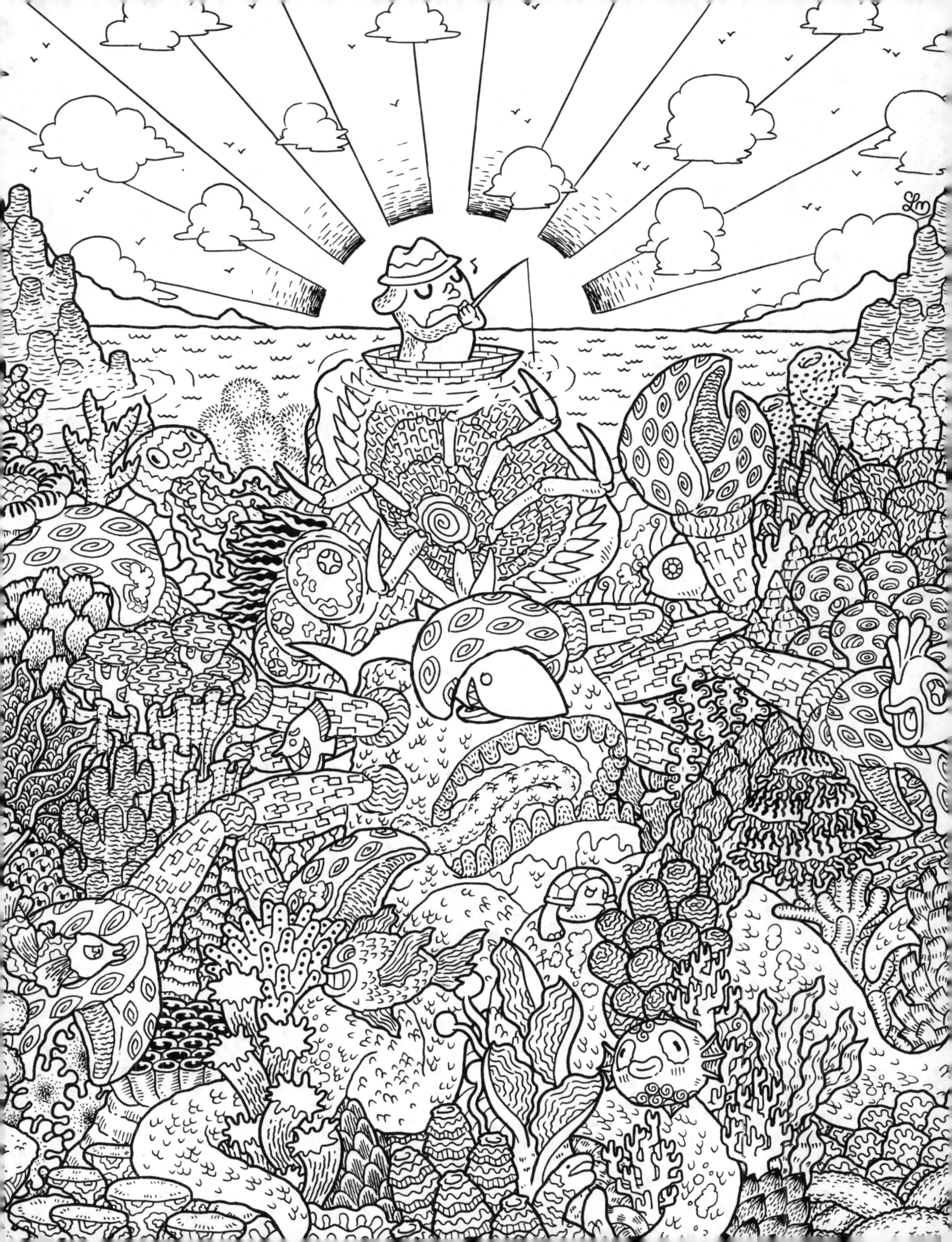

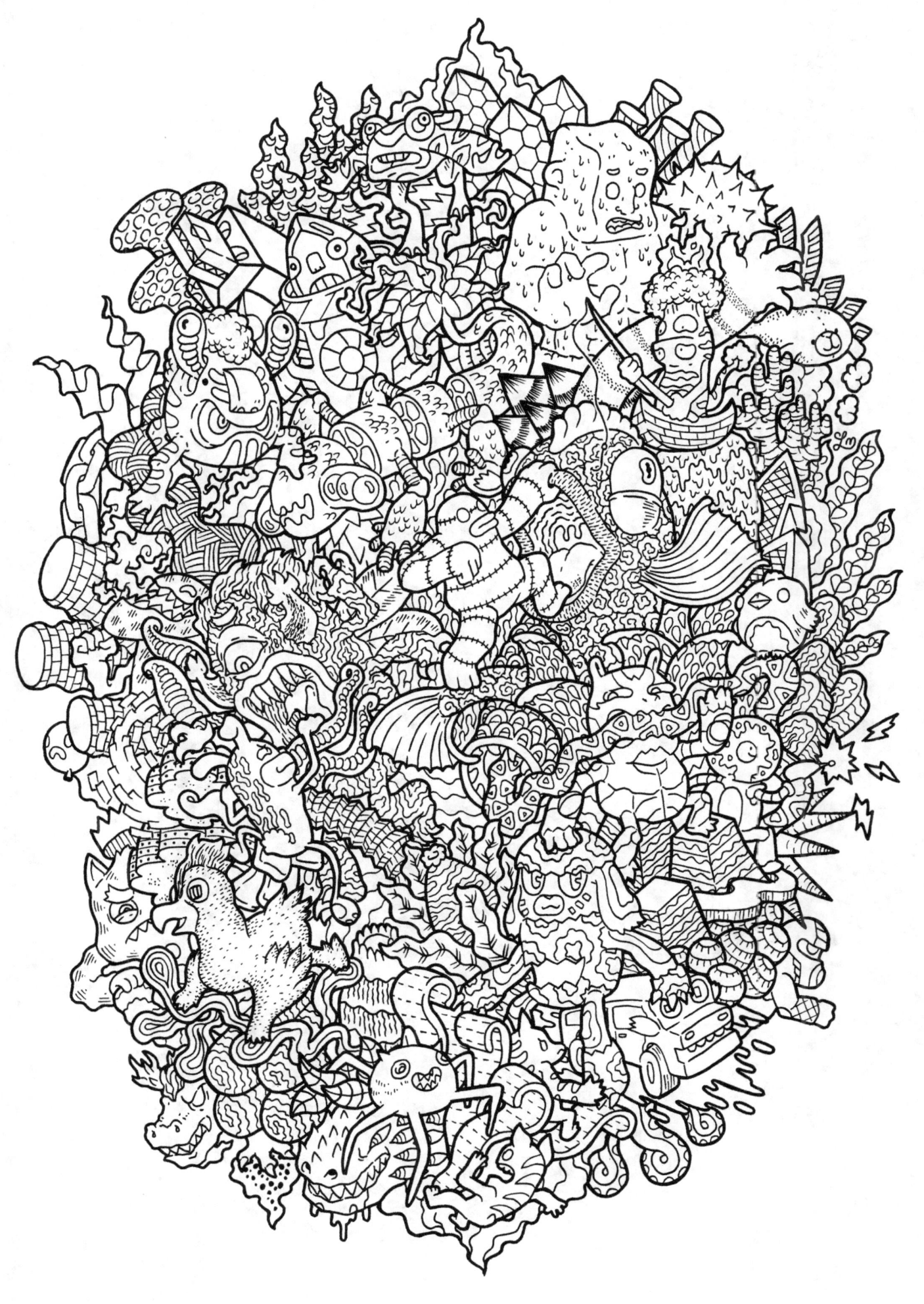

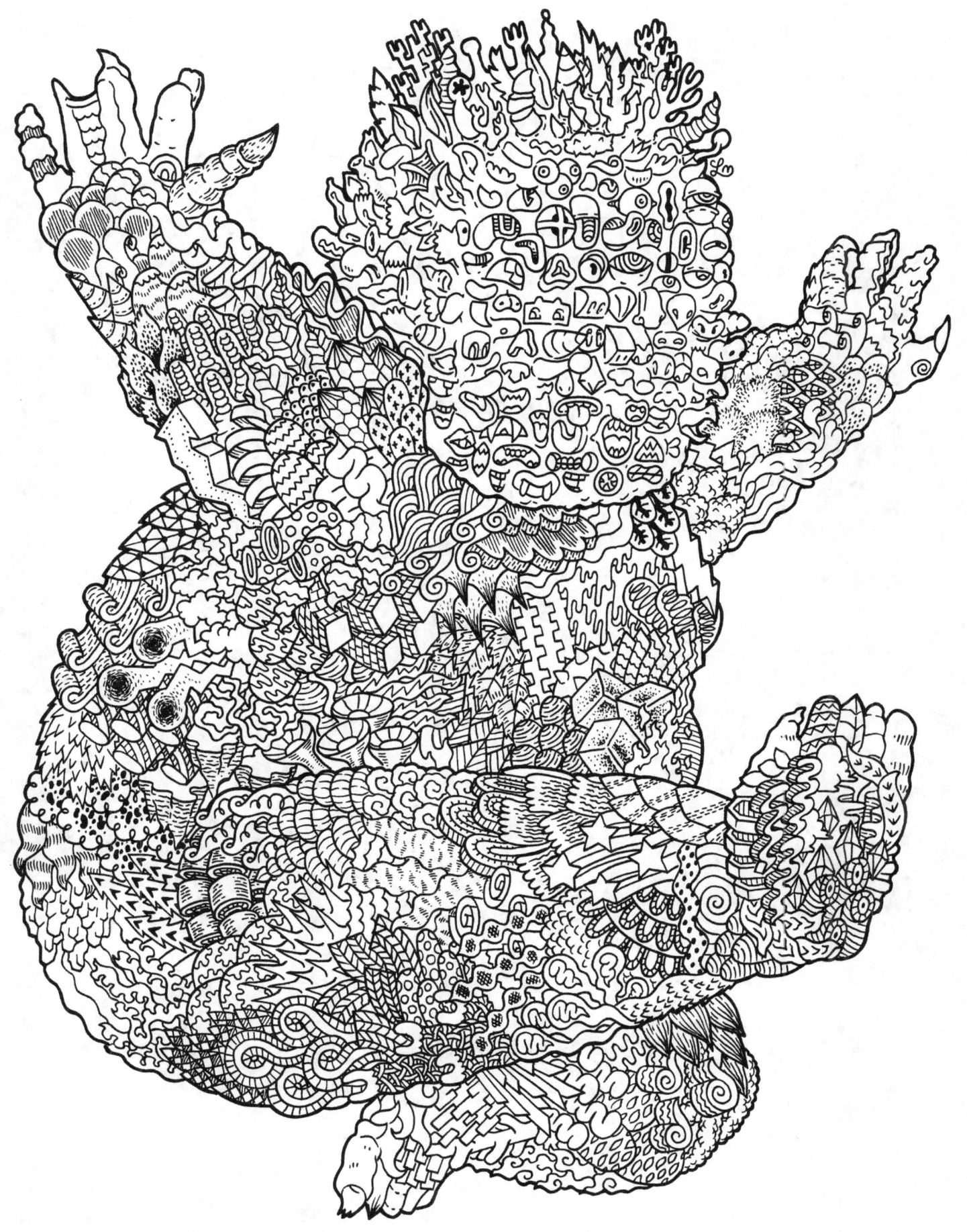

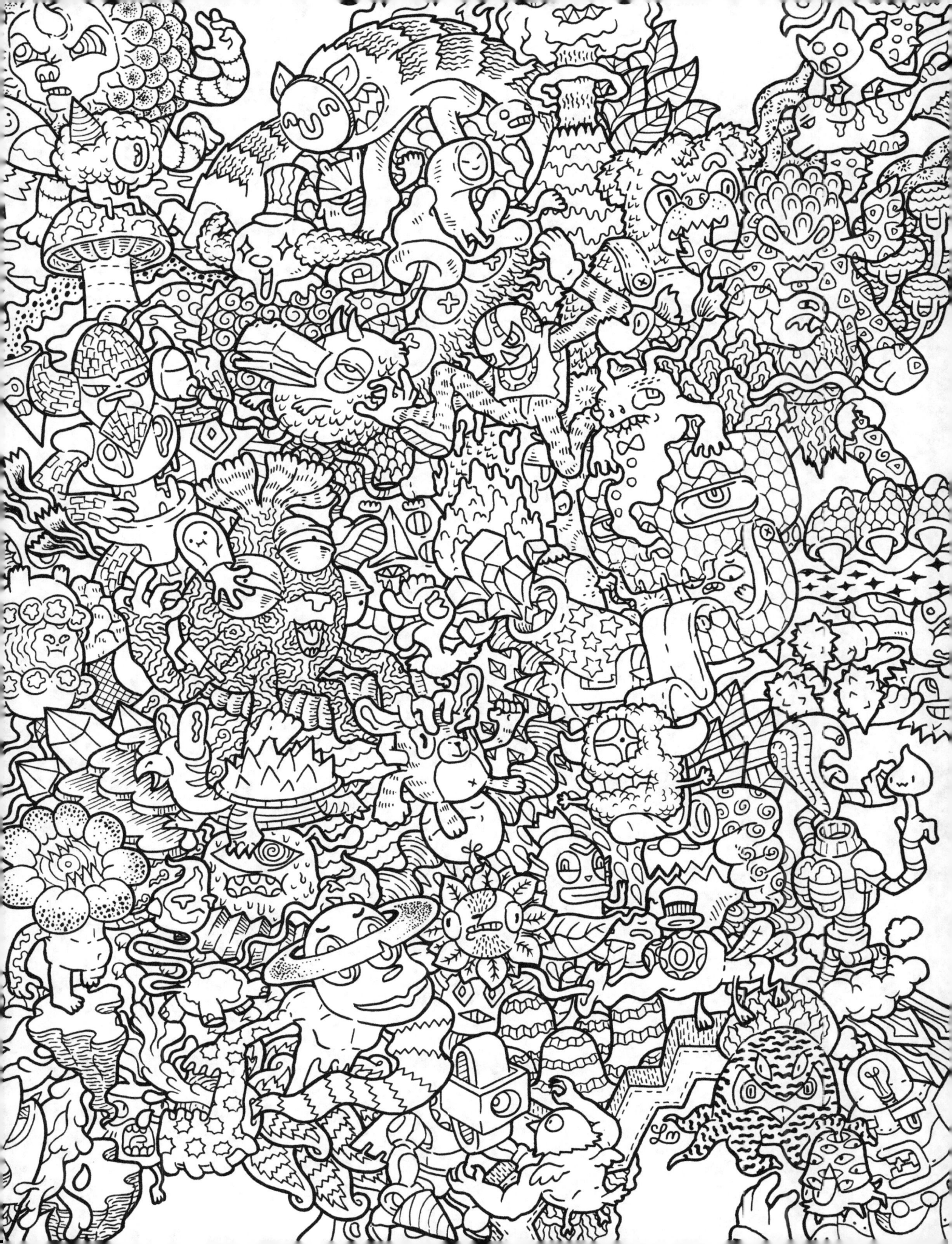

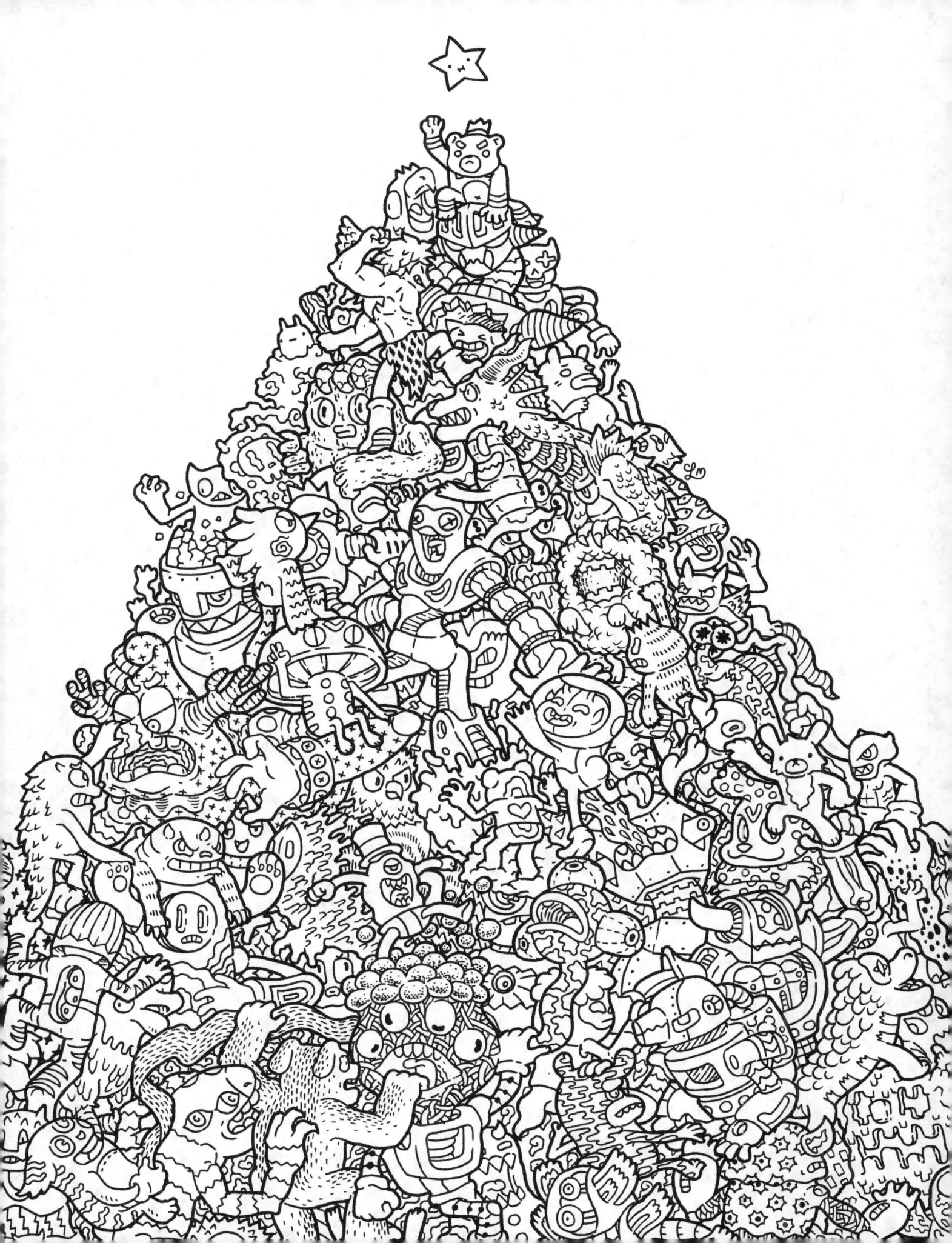

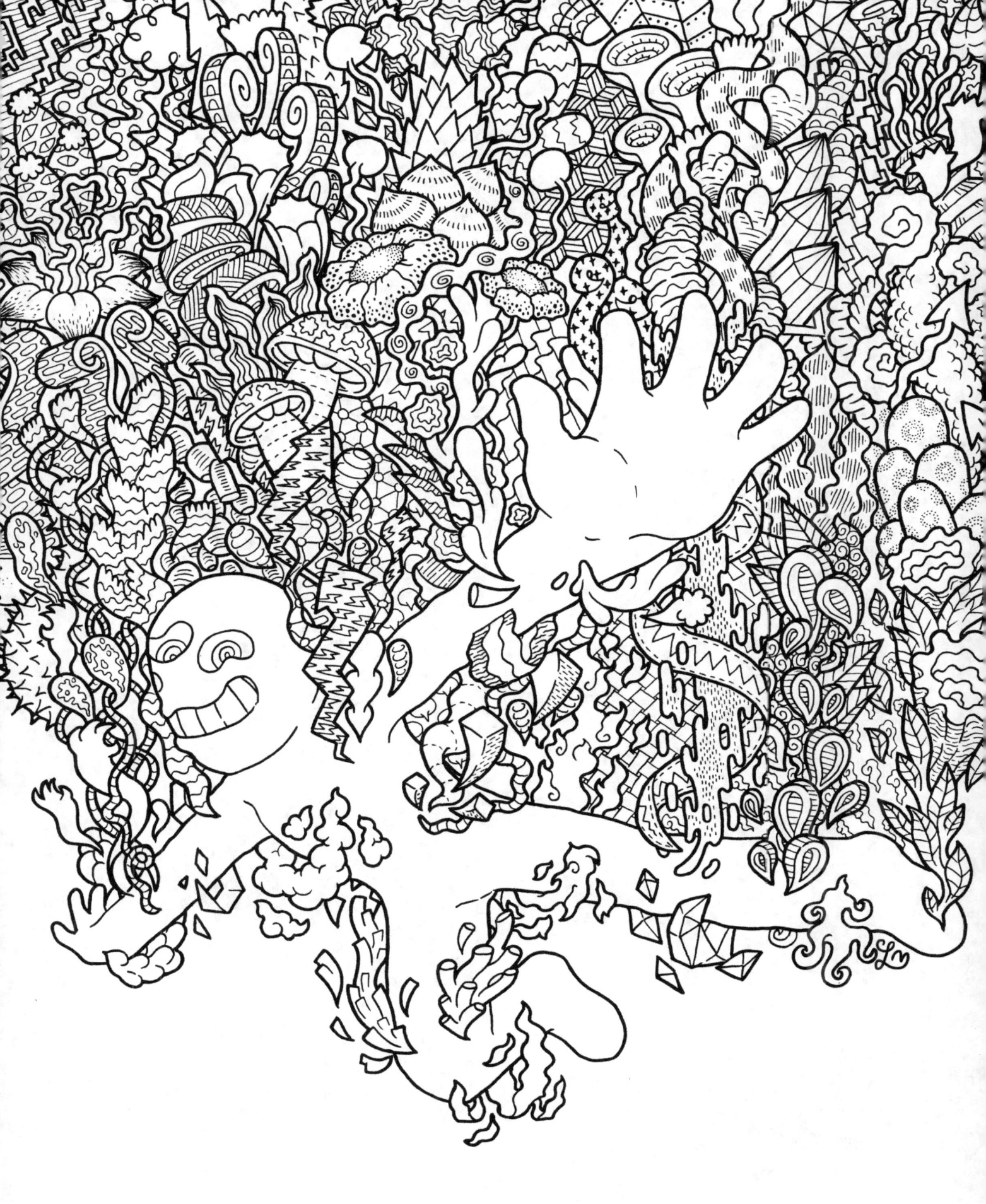

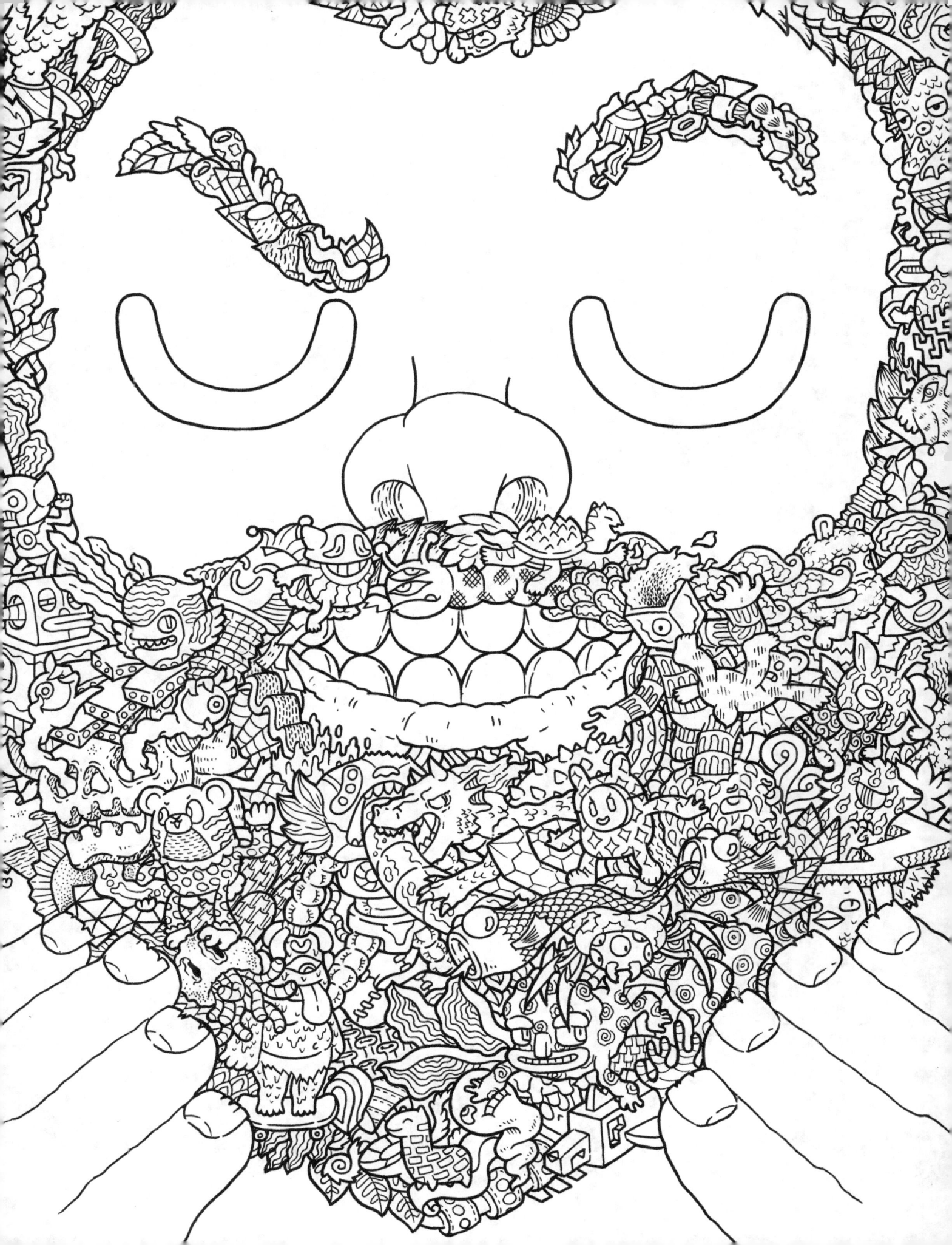

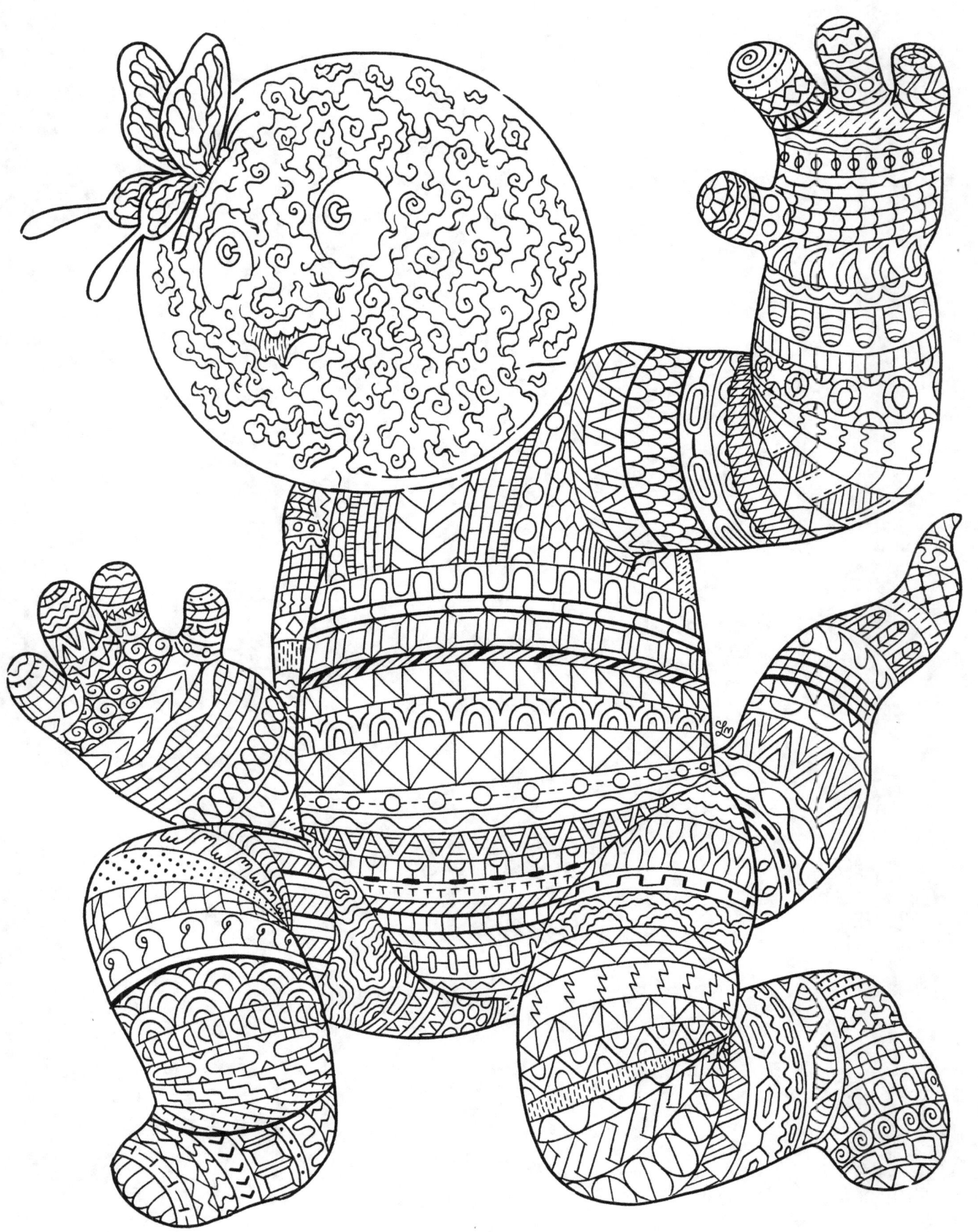

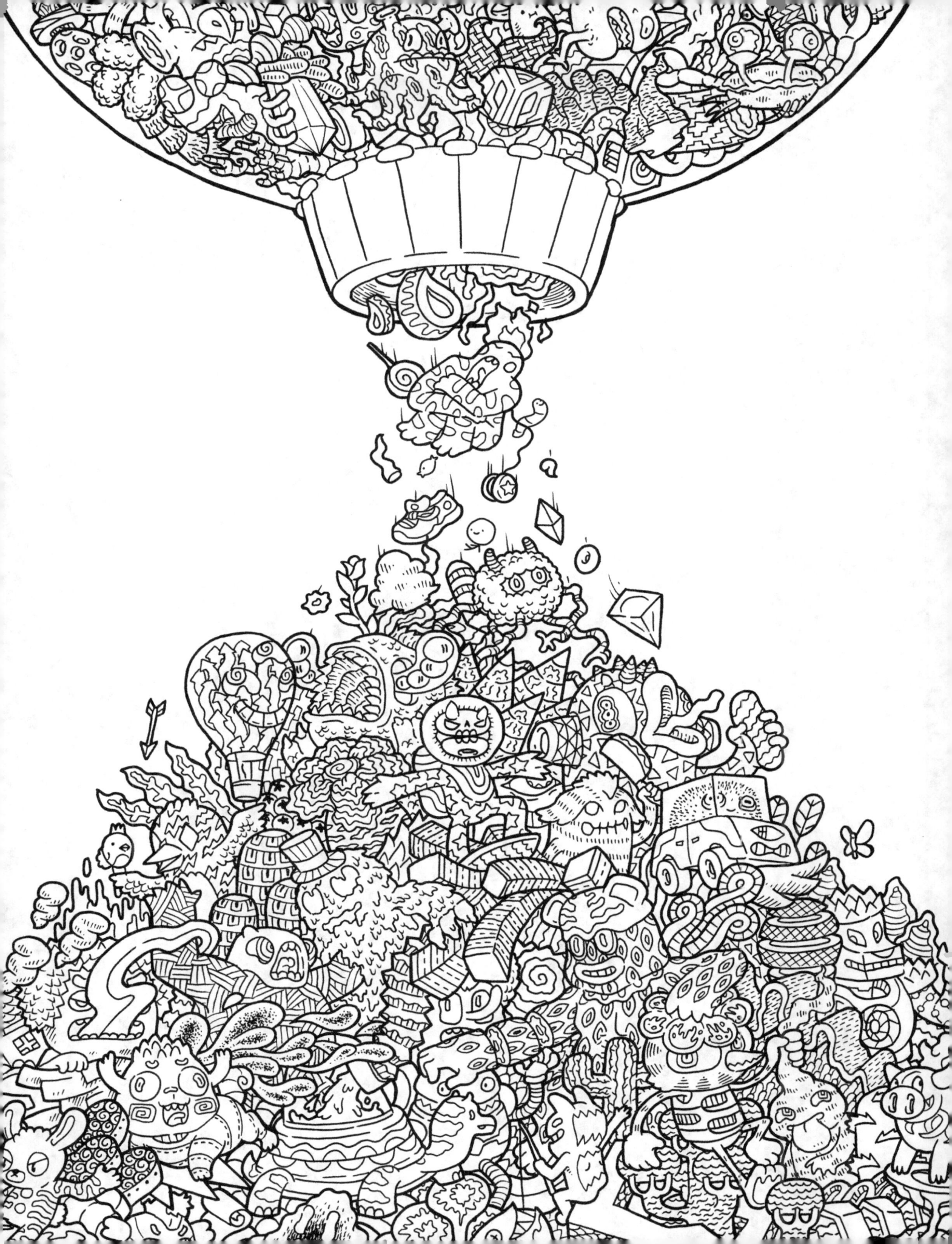

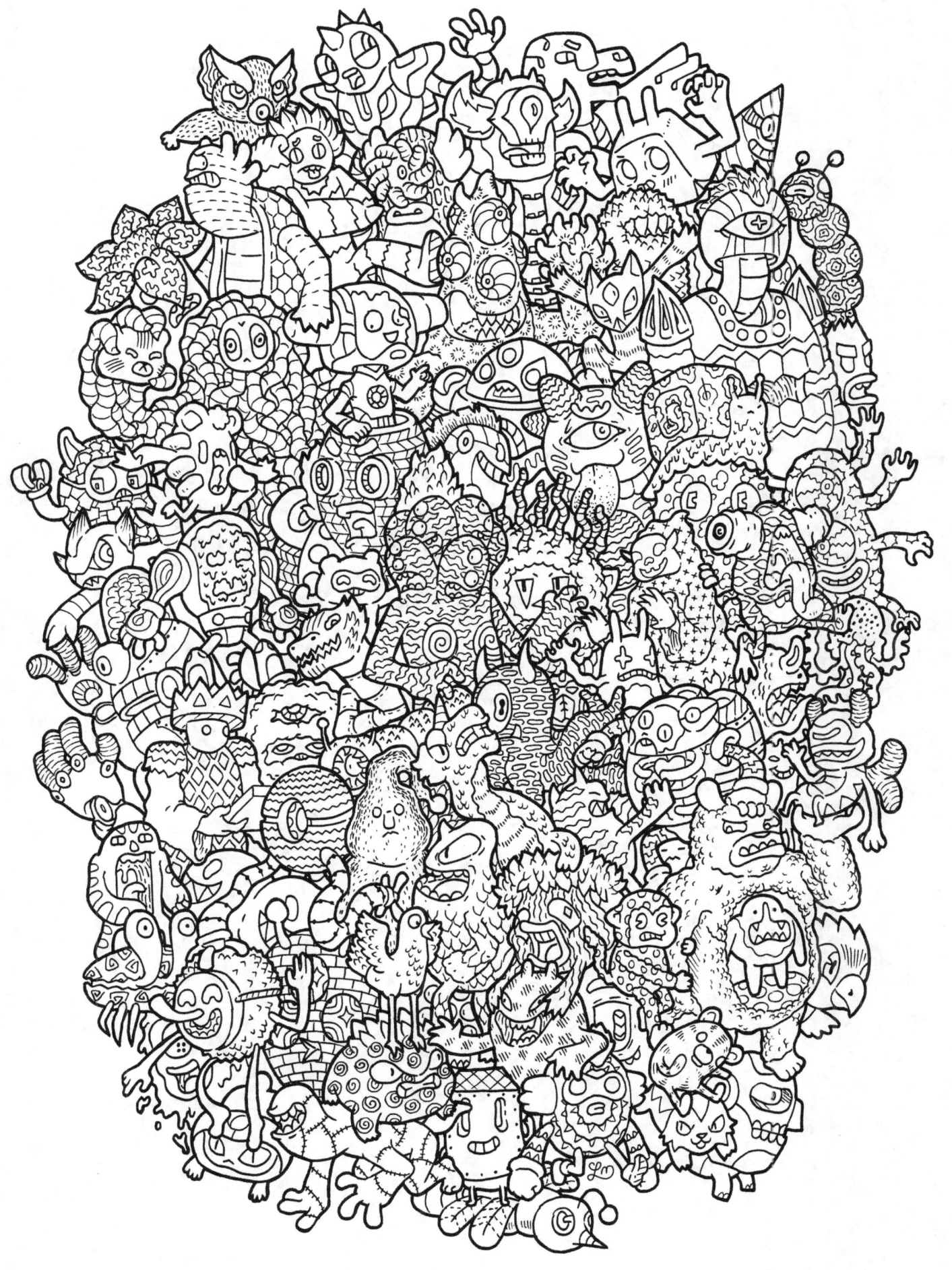

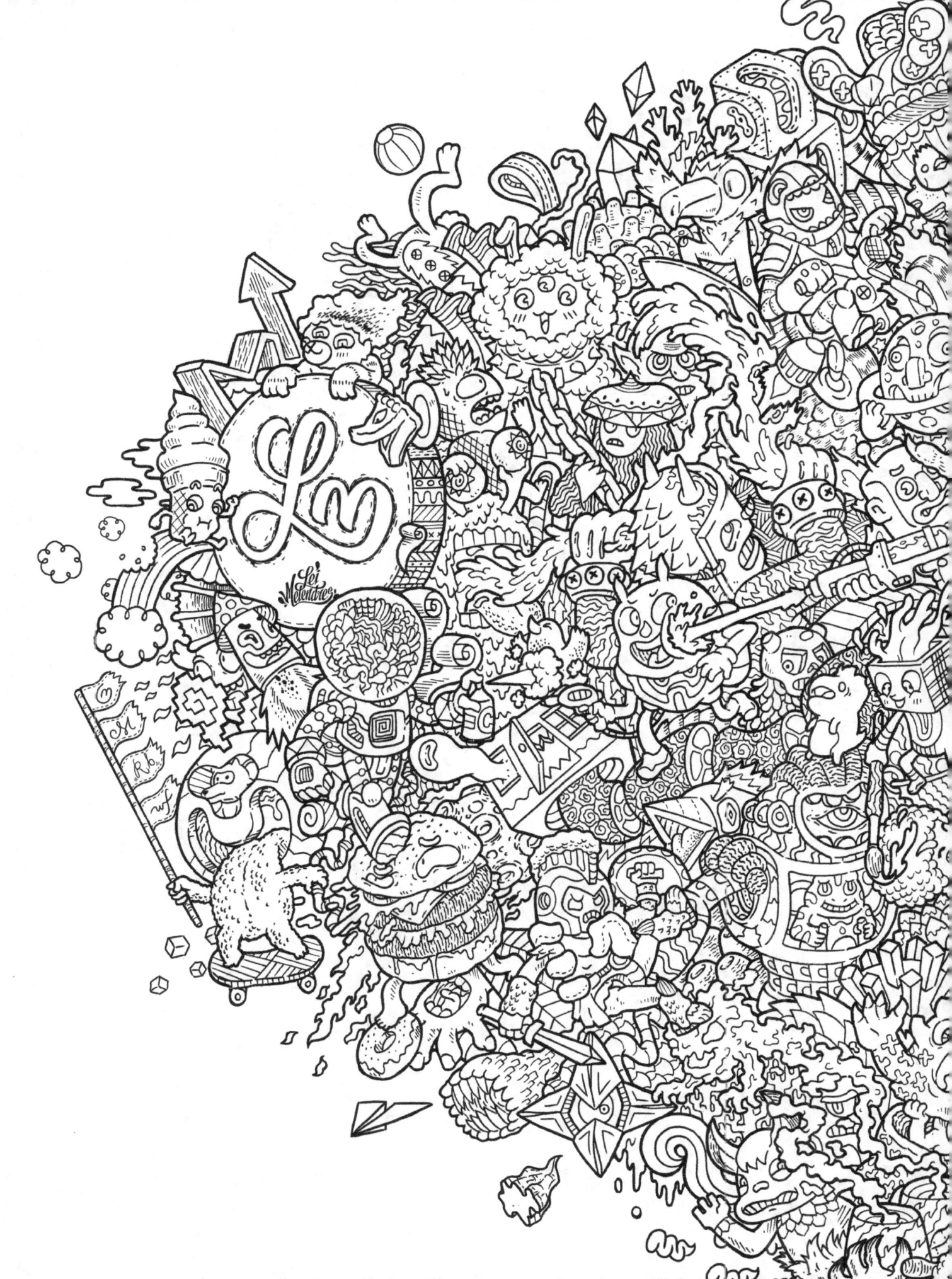

More about the illustrator Lei Melendres.

Manila-based Lei Melendres a.k.a Leight is a 25-year old freelance illustrator and professional doodle artist whose works have been featured in different esteemed publications (books, magazines, newspaper), art and design websites, and local and international galleries and exhibits. Lei provides a general mix of creativity by serving local and foreign clients using "Infinity Mix", his style that describes the intensity of endless details and elements interacting together to form a scene. Doodle Art is his technique and point of reference where it defines repetition, patterns, monsters, animals, unimaginable creatures, the unknown, and other weird stuffs.

Instagram: @lei_melendres #HeyLeight
Facebook: fb.com/iamleight
Behance: behance.net/leight
DeviantART: lei-melendres.deviantart.com

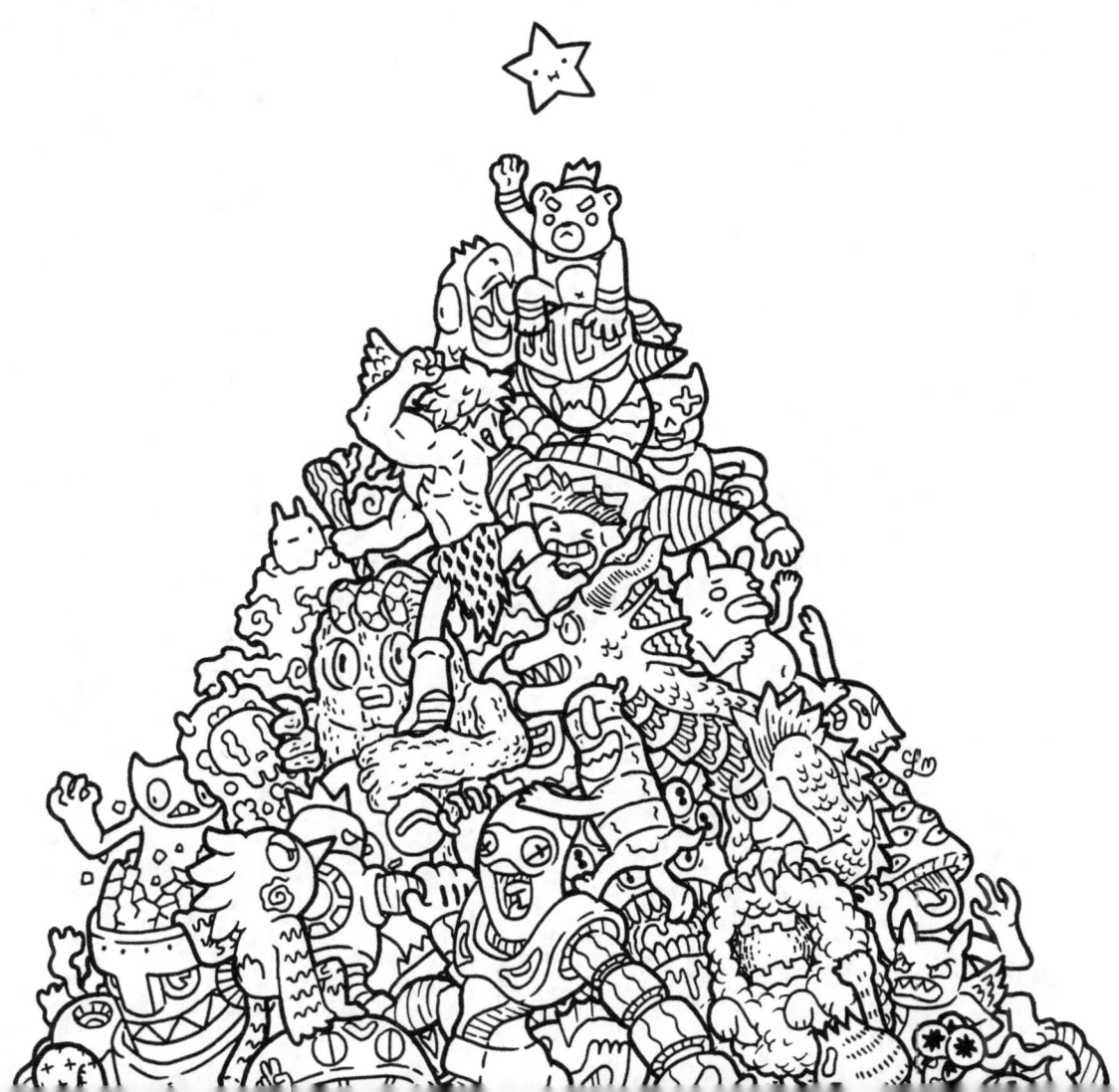

www.ingramcontent.com/pod-product-compliance
Lightning Source LLC
Chambersburg PA
CBHW080823180526

45168CB00006B/2559